DAVIDA

DAVIDA

MODEL & MISTRESS OF
AUGUSTUS SAINT-GAUDENS

KAREN INGALLS

*To Michael, Richard, and David Crislip—my three sons,
who are the great-great-grandsons of Augustus Saint-Gaudens
and Davida Johnson Clark.*

CONTENTS

PREFACE

Davida is the love story of my great-grandparents: Augustus Saint-Gaudens, one of the most recognized sculptors of the nineteenth and early twentieth centuries, and his mistress, Albertina Hultgren, aka Davida Johnson Clark. Though it is known that Augustus was involved with other women from time to time, his love affair with Albertina lasted many years, until his death in 1907. They had one child, Louis Paul Clark, my grandfather.

Little is known about Albertina. She was born in Sweden and was never married. She lived in New York City; Darien, Connecticut; and Arlington, New Jersey. She changed her name and was Augustus's model for several of his sculptures. Therefore, most of this book is fiction and a creation of what I believe is a beautiful and sad love story.

My grandfather did not talk about his mother, father, or his upbringing. Growing up in the 1890s, he was considered a "bastard child," which left a scar for the rest of his life. He was devoted to his mother, though. He was a quiet gentleman who worked hard to provide for his family. He had few friends, in fear of them learning about the circumstances of his birth. In 1958, at the age of sixty-nine, he died from an aneurysm just nine months after his beloved wife passed away.

It is with great regret that my father and his brother destroyed all the love letters between my great-grandparents. Many years later, my father moaned, "Why were we so stupid and selfish to do such a thing?"

I have the base relief, or large medallion, called *Novy*, which Augustus made of my grandfather when he was about three years old.

This piece of art holds many secrets I wish it could tell me.

I wrote *Davida* in the first person because I feel a strong connection to Albertina (Davida), my great-grandmother. I want the reader to know her as a kind, gentle, beautiful young woman who unconditionally loved Augustus and did her best to raise their son to become an equally kind and gentle man.

In my research, I found different interpretations, dates, and credits regarding the various sculptures I describe in this book. However, I did not find that these variations in details took away from the importance or beauty of the sculptures or the love story itself.

In writing this book, it is *not* my intention to hurt those descendants of Augustus and his wife, Augusta Saint-Gaudens. Though we are distantly related, there has been no communication between the two families, which I regret. I hope someday we can communicate with one another.

ACKNOWLEDGMENTS

My gratitude to the following for assisting me with research for this book:

John Dryfought, former curator of the Saint-Gaudens National Historic Site

Dr. Henry Duffy, current curator of the Saint-Gaudens National Historic Site

Viviane Jullien-Palletier, president, Association les amis d'Augustus Saint-Gaudens

Christine Bories, secretary, Association les amis d'Augustus Saint-Gaudens

Francoise Sarradet, Association les amis d'Augustus Saint-Gaudens, and cousin

Thayer Tolles, curator at Metropolitan Museum of Art, New York City

Monica Eklund Abelsted, family history research

CHAPTER 1

NEW ADVENTURE

1876

It was spring 1876 when Mother and I began our journey aboard a White Star steamship sailing from our native Sweden to the United States. I was fourteen years old. My father had unexpectedly died the previous year, and my mother, Alma, and I were going to a new country to live with her sister and husband.

Our journey started when my father, Gustaf Hultgren, was fatally injured in a timber accident. We lived on a small farm where Papa gathered wood for his family and for the local craftsmen who built furniture, boats, and houses. My father was highly skilled and understood the dangers of his trade, but a tragic accident happened that one fateful day.

I was raised in the small village of Stora Blåsjön in Strömsund, Sweden, where the land is mainly filled with beautiful spruce and pine trees and several lakes. I had experience being on the waters of our lakes but not a vast ocean. Now the trip aboard the steamer bound for New York City was long and arduous, with rough seas and rain almost daily.

We were two women traveling alone, so some people, especially women, looked upon us with suspicion. Men looked upon us in other ways.

One day, I pointed to a group of men with beards, leathery skin, and stained and torn clothing. I asked Mother, "Why are those men over there staring at us?"

"My sweet Albertina, it is not polite to point. But do not pay any attention to those men. They mean no harm. They are merely travelers, like us."

I clutched my mother's hand tightly. Moving ever closer to her, I said, "They frighten me. I wish Papa was here."

Mother's beauty, graceful features, and fine figure brought attention from men wherever she went, but their flirtations were met with austere and cold blue eyes. She had long blonde hair that she swept into a twist and fastened with a long barrette. Her nose was small and thin, sitting between two high cheekbones that gave her a special elegance. Her slim face tapered down to lips that always had a slight smile, and her blue eyes danced like diamonds on the water.

Once people got to know us and heard our story, they were kind and friendly. I made friends with Harry and Monica, who had lived in the same neighborhood of Stockholm. They had been friends almost since birth. Their families chose to seek freedom and employment in America after learning of the many opportunities from relatives who had immigrated there earlier.

Without hesitation, Monica asked, "Why are you and your mother traveling alone to America? Where is your father?"

Monica's blonde pigtails were tied in place with two faded blue ribbons hung halfway down her back. She was an outgoing, lively spirit always chattering in a very animated manner. Everyone liked her.

Harry had a tall and lanky body. His arms were so long, I imagined he could reach up and touch the moon. He was the opposite of Monica in personality. When he was nervous or excited, he ran his left hand through his thick and wavy light-brown hair.

"Monica, you are too abrupt," Harry quickly interjected. "And besides, it is none of your business." He turned to me. "I am sorry. Sometimes Monica speaks before she thinks."

With her hands on her hips, Monica asserted, "I am not being rude.

I just asked a simple question."

We were outside on the deck enjoying our first sunny day at sea. It felt good to be out from the confines of the steerage, where the air was thick. I looked at my new friends and decided to share what happened to my dear papa.

"One day, Papa was in the forest with his best friend, Henrik, cutting down trees. A tree fell on Papa, and he died."

I looked at Monica and Harry, observing their shocked reactions, before I continued.

"I will never forget that day. It was October 10, 1875. Henrik brought Papa's broken body on the wagon that would normally hold the logs."

I started to cry, the hot tears running down my cheeks. My new friends quietly sat and waited while I composed myself.

"Mother and I are going to live with my aunt and uncle in New Jersey. They are the only family we have in America."

The wind suddenly began to blow cold air. Dark clouds moved across the once-clear sky. Harry and Monica both said how sorry they were, then quickly excused themselves. I am sure my story about Papa upset them—or perhaps they did not believe me.

I found a place near a lifeboat where I could sit alone and undisturbed. The memories of that fateful day continued to fill my mind. I wiped away more tears, recalling Henrik's words as he conveyed the news to Mother and me.

"I was cutting down a tree. I thought I was a safe distance away from Gustaf, who was just beginning to chop down a slightly smaller pine. Suddenly there was a loud noise of breaking branches and splintering trees." Henrik put his hand to his forehead, shook his head back and forth. "Just as I swung the axe one last time, I realized Gustaf was too close. I couldn't stop the axe in time. I'm so sorry."

Mother consoled him. "Take your time, dear friend, but do tell us everything." Turning to me, she instructed, "Albertina, go in the house and get Henrik a cup of coffee."

My legs seemed stuck in the ground. It took great effort to walk the few steps into our cabin. When I returned, Henrik and Mother were sitting on the front steps.

The coffee and Mother's kindness helped Henrik continue his account. "The larger pine fell to the ground, almost as if it just couldn't hold itself up any longer. The upper trunk fell on Gustaf's chest. I'm sure it quickly crushed out all life. I pushed and pulled until I could finally roll it off him. It took me a long time, but eventually I was able to pull my dear friend Gustaf free."

He looked from Mother to me. "I am not as big and strong as Gustaf, yet I found the strength to move the tree and lift him up onto the wagon. Where did that strength come from? I know there was some kind of magic in the forest helping me."

Mother and I did not say anything, but we looked at each other knowing that God, angels, and elves would want our beloved papa and husband brought back to his family, whom he loved so much.

I began to sob, envisioning my dear papa's strong body lying lifeless. No longer would I hear his boisterous laughter and vibrant voice, nor feel his strong arms hugging me. I stared at the wagon with Papa's body under the large canvas cover the two men had used for years for their cut lumber.

With each passing day on the ship, the weather became colder and harsher. We spent our long days confined in the small steel rooms below the promenade. I told Harry and Monica more about Papa.

As I related to them, Papa loved the spirit of the forest. Each tree was special in its own way, whether it had majestically stood in the forest for many years or was a new sapling that had yet to put its roots down deep. When I shared this, Monica and Harry looked at each other with little smiles and raised eyebrows, showing me they did not believe in such spirits.

I explained how the long dark nights and short cold days of that winter were lonely and empty for both Mother and me. The stars did not shine as bright, the fireplace was not as warm, and the supper table seemed empty. Yet we both felt his presence in mysterious and magical ways we could not explain. We found comfort just knowing he was with us in some unknown way.

When Mother's sister, Ingrid, first invited us to come to America, we discussed it as if Papa were sitting in his chair, ready to give his opinion. Mother knew it would be very difficult to earn enough money for us to remain in our home. We lived on a very small farm, where we raised two milking cows, some chickens, and vegetables to sell to the local townspeople and markets.

A few years before they married, Papa had cleared about one acre surrounded by the beautiful forests and built a small wooden house in preparation to marry my mother, whom he had loved for many years. "No man should invite a woman to share his life if he cannot provide a house of her own," was his credo.

The house was made from logs felled by my father's ax and layered with mud and pine needles between each log for insulation and strength. On the inside, he rubbed pine oil into each log until it had the clarity and sheen that satisfied his artistic eye.

Once he finished the house, he went to my grandfather Hallgren to ask for my mother's hand in marriage. Everyone knew Alma and Gustaf would one day marry. They had been best friends since they first met as youngsters, and over the years that friendship had developed into a deep love.

Two months after Papa's death, Mother's family encouraged her to accept a wedding proposal from a distant widower with three children. But she did not want to marry the kind gentleman.

"I do not love him," she declared.

Grandmother Hallgren tried to reassure Mother that someday she would marry again.

Mother answered, "Why would I ever want to marry again when I have already loved and married my soul mate?"

Our ocean voyage took eight days. Every chance I had I spent on deck, leaning against the railing and marveling at the beauty of the blue water with the white foam leaving a trail behind the ship. I tried to imagine what kinds of fish and creatures lived beneath the water. Were there beings in the water, as there are spirits in the forest? Did sea älvas guide those ships of good intent? Did evil serpents and monsters cause other ships and passengers to sink to the ocean floor?

Harry and Monica laughed at my inquisitive and fanciful thoughts. They liked it when I shared Papa's tales of the forest, but then they would say, "Just remember, you silly girl, your papa was just telling stories."

I told Mother about my thoughts when I looked out at the ocean. She would just smile and say, "You are so like your papa."

Mother and I met Mrs. Arleigh Clark, a woman from Stockholm who was also a recent widow. She was traveling to Ontario, Canada, to live with her daughter. Mrs. Clark had a smile and a sparkle in her eyes that captured our hearts immediately.

When Mother shared the story about Papa's death, Mrs. Clark said, "I am sure it was the forest beings who helped your friend Henrik raise the tree off your husband's chest." She looked at us and asked, "You do believe in them, don't you?"

I learned more from Mrs. Clark about the mysteries, legends, and magic of elves, älvas, dwarves, and gnomes. She also planted the seeds of believing in a loving and kind God, not one who is harsh and judgmental.

She also helped Mother when they talked about their new lives without their husbands.

"Sometimes life seems harsh," Mrs. Clark assured, "but there is a reason for everything. I know my dear husband is with me and that brings me great comfort."

Mother nodded her head in agreement.

CHAPTER 2

NEW LAND

1876

One very early morning, I awoke to shouts of joy as our ship neared the old fort Castle Garden in the New World. The fort sat on a rocky islet in the bay about three hundred yards from the southern tip of Manhattan Island. The large wooden building with its prominent rotunda was the first port opened to immigrants. Its massiveness was quite overwhelming and spectacular. The site was often referred to as the "Golden Door."

An officer dressed in a blue uniform with a hat held in place by a chin strap boarded our ship. He checked for any ill passengers, wrote the names of those who had died during the journey, and noted the number of passengers and the general cleanliness of the ship. Once our luggage was weighed, we were transported to a tugboat that took us to the pier.

I was most frightened with all the confusion. Passengers bumped into one another. Officials ordered us around with scowls on their faces, leaving me feeling most unwelcome in this new land.

If Mother were frightened, she did not appear so. She held her head high and looked the officers squarely in the eyes as she followed their instructions.

I tightly clutched her hand. "I am afraid they will send us back to the ship to return to Sweden," I told her. "Or even worse, that they will arrest us and lock us up in jail!"

Mother whispered, "Everything is okay. Do not worry, my child. I have all the papers Aunt Ingrid said we would need."

We were then directed to a medical officer, who quickly examined us for any disease. From there, we went into a separate room for women and were told to bathe with soap and water. I was quite embarrassed but followed Mother's example.

Once we were considered clean, we entered a large rotunda. An official pointed us toward an area for those who did not speak English. We tried to stay close to the people we had come to know aboard the ship, finding some comfort in the familiarity of language and friendship. But some of us became separated as we made our way through the lines and stations and merged with passengers from another ship.

I listened to and watched the hundreds of people surrounding us. Like us, they carried their satchels, suitcases, or boxes of possessions. There were so many colors, sizes, and languages. Different dresses and suits. Young and old. Families and a few traveling alone. I wanted to know more about them and their stories. What brought them here? Was it a sudden death, as in our situation? Were they running away *from* or *to* something? Could they speak any English? Where would they live in America?

The line was long and slow, but finally we were standing in front of a clerk sitting behind a small desk. He asked Mother our names, nationality, where we had lived, where we were going to live, and names of relatives with whom we would be staying. I was impressed with how well the agent and Mother were able to communicate with each other.

We finally departed the building with the other immigrants searching for their families or heading to the nearby trains that would take them to their destinations. Mother scanned the greeting crowd for Ingrid and her husband, Nels. Like the cows we once had on our farm, we were pushed and prodded in the crowd. Somehow people were herded into the welcoming arms of family and friends. I was too big to be carried yet too short to see anything except the chests of strangers, with their different languages, smells, and clothing. It was both frightening and exciting.

Once the crowd thinned out, Mother saw Ingrid waving a colorful kerchief, her arm stretched high above her head. She stood next to Nels, a tall, blond, and slender man. We rushed to them. Soon there was laughter and tears of joy and relief as hugs and kisses were exchanged.

While Mother was a natural beauty, always smiling and effervescent, Ingrid was quiet and shy and looked more like a child herself, with a plain face and short and round body. But both sisters were very kind and generous, and they won friendship and trust quickly.

"What a beautiful young lady you are, Albertina," Ingrid exclaimed as she reached out to hug me. "Welcome. We are so glad you are here."

For a moment I was lost in the arms and bosom of my aunt, who kept repeating words of happiness and excitement.

"You do take after your mother with her beauty. But I also see strength of character from your father."

I curtsied and whispered, "Thank you, ma'am."

We climbed into the open wagon and sat atop our luggage while Nels and Ingrid sat on the front bench. We made our way down dirt roads surrounded by the tall buildings and houses in New York City. Each house was mainly made of brick, with steps leading up to a large wooden door. Just as in Stockholm, the houses were two to three stories high and were connected down the entire block.

Many people were hurrying past one another, brushing shoulders. With heads down, they were determined to reach their destinations without having to acknowledge anyone. The men were mainly dressed in black or gray coats and trousers and wore hats of various proportions. The women's dresses also lacked color. The women strolled more slowly, taking time to stop in front of shop windows or at vendors' carts. Some walked in pairs, their heads leaning toward each other as they were absorbed in conversation.

Street vendors stood by their heavily laden carts and shouted out invitations to see their wares. It was music to my ears to hear these English words spoken with the lilt or rhythm of the vendors' native languages. Here were carts plentiful with fresh fruit and vegetables, bolts of various colors of fabric, and pots, pans, dishes, and utensils. One cart was laden with many books stacked precariously on top of one another. I had never seen so many books, and I longed to stop and look at each one. There was also a woman wearing many gold and silver bracelets, which jingled as she waved her arms high above her head. The skirts of her bright-purple dress flowed in the gentle wind, and her long necklaces bounced up and down on her large chest.

The excitement and hum of activity was intoxicating. Everything was so much bigger, newer, and different from Stockholm. That day I fell in love with America, which was so different from the land I had left a short time ago.

But then all at once, it was as if I had awakened from a dream. I realized I was now truly in a new country and probably would never see Sweden again. The excitement of the city became frightening. I began to long for the quiet whispers of the pine trees, the gentle lapping of the waves on our lakes, and the peaceful sway of the villagers moving to a rhythm sung in their souls. Tears swelled up in my eyes, and I leaned my body close to Mother. I wanted to be in Papa's protective arms and hear his words of assurance that everything would be all right.

Mother patted my knee as if she understood my tears. "Everything will be all right, Albertina. Do not be frightened," she assured me as I looked up into her gentle eyes.

We boarded a ferry that took us across the Hudson River to Hoboken, New Jersey, leaving behind the hurriedness and noise of Manhattan. Hoboken had one main street lined with a mercantile store, a post office, a livery barn, and the inn where Mother would later work. At each end, there were graceful houses with picturesque small gardens, curving paths leading to large and small porches, and lace curtains providing daintiness and privacy to the framed windows.

Hoboken's streets were lined with brick or clapboard homes with green lawns and large porches. As we passed, a few people waved to us and shouted greetings for the day. I saw some men dressed in coveralls, plaid cotton shirts, and wide-brimmed hats sheltering their rough and weathered faces. One woman was seen in a garden, another was walking down a sidewalk with her children, and a couple sat on the porch sorting and preparing various fruits and vegetables. My first impressions of this new country were of busyness, peace, friendliness, and beauty.

Nels and Ingrid's farm was just outside of town, where the beautiful rolling hills were lush with pine and aspen trees. Their red barn housed the dairy cattle, a few horses, and many bales of straw and hay. The white wooden farmhouse had a wide porch on which sat two rocking chairs, and green shutters framed the windows.

The excitement of that first day was soon replaced by weariness. My eyes became heavy and could not be kept open. I do not remember how I got into bed.

I awoke to the early rays of sunshine and the sound of my mother's voice.

"Albertina, rise and shine, you sleepyhead.

Nels and Ingrid married in 1857, and they lived with Nel's family in Stora Blåsjön for a year, helping his father run the farm, before immigrating to America in 1858. They settled in Lynn, Massachusetts, where Nels worked on a dairy farm and Ingrid worked as a cook for the local hotel. They lived frugally for four years, saving every penny they could, until one day in 1862, they bought the small farm in Hoboken, New Jersey.

Their farm was surrounded by a beautiful forest, which reminded me of Stora Blåsjön. They had dairy cows, two goats, chickens, pigs, and about one hundred acres of cropland for soybeans and corn. They also had a small grove of apple trees from which Ingrid made delicious apple cider, pies, and sauce. Nels made wood carvings of ducks and birds, and Ingrid knitted sweaters, mittens, scarves, and hats so beautifully detailed in Swedish patterns. They sold these items at local fairs, to merchants in Manhattan, and at Hoboken's city square every Saturday.

In her youth, Ingrid had always hoped to marry her childhood sweetheart, Nels Petersson, and someday have children to love and bring up on the Hallgren family farm. However, fate stepped in when dysentery swiftly struck the Hallgren family when she was twelve and Mother was ten. It took the lives of their parents and their grandmother Hallgren. Ingrid became sick with this deadly disease, but she survived—perhaps due to her youth or fortitude. Or perhaps it was in God's plan, according to some people. For some reason, Mother did not contract this too-often fatal disease. Their uncle and aunt became their guardians, and the sisters went to live with them in a neighboring village. Within a year, their uncle sold their parents' beloved farm to a neighbor, destroying one of Ingrid's dreams to live there for the rest of her life.

Ingrid was never able to have children, yet it did not stop her from volunteering at the local church helping young mothers, the elderly, or the ill in any way she could. Nels would tell her she should be a nurse.

"You are always thinking of other people first," he would say.

"I am quite content with my life as it is," Ingrid would reply with a smile while looking up into Nels's eyes. "I do not need to be a nurse or anything else. Being your wife is all I want to be."

Nels was tall, slender, quiet, and immediately liked by everyone. He did not try to push his ideas on anyone, argue politics, nor imbibe in drinking. He worked hard and faithfully in whatever job. His only vice was his love to smoke, and there was always a cigarette in his mouth. But he sometimes coughed so hard that Ingrid would be frightened for his well-being. She tried to persuade him to go to a doctor, but he refused saying, "It is just a cough, my dear."

Aunt Ingrid was most instrumental in teaching English to Mother and me. The new language sounded harsh and loud compared to the musical rhythm of my native Swedish. But I quickly picked up the strange language because it was everywhere. It was written in every book, in every newspaper, and on every storefront, and it was spoken by all the townspeople. English settlers founded the town of Hoboken, but immigrants from Germany, Norway, and Sweden also made it their home, so the new language was heard with different accents given.

Ingrid took a position as the housekeeper for an up-and-coming sculptor in New York City by the name of Augustus Saint-Gaudens. Sometimes Ingrid took lunches over to one of Saint-Gaudens's studios. She admired his work and was overwhelmed with the beauty of the small and large sculptures she saw. She often entertained us with her impersonations of Mr. Saint-Gaudens working on a sculpture, singing in a beautiful tenor voice, stopping only to give new instructions to his workers. Ingrid would take the ferry across the Hudson River every day and then walk the short blocks to the Saint-Gaudens's home, which she described in detail of beauty and orderliness.

"Mrs. Saint-Gaudens is friendly and well mannered. She is a true lady but is stern and cold—often talking quite loud due to her deafness."

Mother found work as a cook at the local Whispering Pines Inn. She would leave before sunrise and come home after dark every day except Sunday, which was her only day off. I missed her when she was gone. One night before bedtime, I complained about how I saw her only briefly each evening, but she reprimanded me.

"Albertina, you should just be grateful that I am strong enough to work to put food on the table, a roof over your pretty head, and a warm bed to sleep in each night. Let me hear no more words of selfishness from you."

"I am sorry, Mother," I whispered, fighting the tears swelling in my eyes. I knew I had upset her.

After a moment, Mother sat down and put her arms around me. "I am sorry too. But this is the way our life will be for a while. Thank God we have Nels and Ingrid here to help us. And I do thank God every day that I have you, my little angel."

I soaked in the comfort and love that flowed from Mother as we sat and rocked in each other's arms. That night I learned a lesson by which I lived the rest of my life: sometimes life requires hard sacrifices, but strength of body, character, and family gets you through those times.

I helped Ingrid in the large vegetable garden and with the flower-beds in front of the house. Gardening had been one of my favorite activities on our farm in Sweden. I had always loved the warmth of the soil—even when it was still cool during the early spring days. Either kneeling or bending down, I worked clumps loose in my hands, parted the soil to make a hole, then moved it back around the plant or seeds.

This was a time when I would be lost in my thoughts, and I'd feel a special communion with God and the earth. The plants and crops were special gifts from God that were to be handled with love and tenderness. They were like newborn children to be nurtured and cared for as they grew. Then in spring, watching the plants pushing through the still-cool soil was exciting. And in the summer, the crops and beauty of the flowers was a true joy.

Most of the time, I walked to school. When snow blanketed the landscape, I skied along the road, often following Mother's ski tracks from a few hours earlier.

There was steamboat service from Hoboken to New York City and trains from the south and west ending in Jersey City and Hoboken. The trains with their massive engines were exciting for me, and I loved to hear their whistles blow.

I grew to love Hoboken, its people, and its culture. In school, I quickly improved my English and adapted to the school's program, even though I was not a very good student.

The forests in New Jersey were beautiful, but at first they did not appear to have the same magic as the woodlands of Sweden. That saddened me. Perhaps it was just that I missed the wonderful stories my papa would tell about his forests adventures. Or perhaps it was really because I missed my friends back home and the familiarity of Swedish customs, language, food, and music. I walked among the trees and along the river, often hoping to hear nature talk to me as it had so often with Papa in Stora Blåsjön.

CHAPTER 3

HOBOKEN

1877–78

I walked Main Street to and from school. Toward the end of the block, a yellow house with white trim especially captured my attention with its scrolled porch and bannister. In the spring, potted geraniums sat on each side of the two steps leading to the white-painted porch. There on the porch, two white wicker chairs rested around a small round wicker table.

When it was warm, I often saw a sweet-faced lady named Maria Louise Johnson sitting in one of those chairs, smiling kindly and greeting me with a hello. She had beautiful gray hair that shone like honey in the sunshine. It was gracefully pulled back in a soft twist at the nape of her neck. Small ringlets framed her face, and her pronounced widow's peak seemed to say, "Look at me."

One wintry day, she was not out on her porch, but as I passed by, she opened her front door and invited me in for a cup of hot tea.

"You must be cold, my dear. Come in, and let's get to know each other."

That was the first of many days we spent together. I found a trusted friend and someone I wanted to be just like: kind, beautiful, and friendly.

Mrs. Johnson insisted I call her Maria, just as most of the townspeople did. At first it seemed disrespectful to address an elder in such an informal way. But I soon learned it was a sign of affection once permission was granted.

I often talked about my papa with Maria. One day I shared a time when Papa came home to tell about an encounter with a doe. The doe had stood as still as a statue staring at him with big brown eyes that seemed to penetrate his soul. Time seemed to stand still, allowing these two souls to communicate and live in peace.

"I knew that doe was telling me to be on my way. She meant no harm to me, so I must not harm her. She had a young newborn to care for," Papa had related one brisk fall evening. "I told the doe I also had a child to raise. I understood there can be perils in the woods. I told her, 'Do not fear me, for I am only a simple woodsman out here to cut some timber to sell.'"

Maria smiled. "I think you might be a lot like your father. Your eyes show a true compassion for life, and you have an energy, or aura, that seeks the same magic in people as your father did in the forest." She took a sip of her tea. After a pause, she went on, "Life can be cruel. But Albertina, you have the gift to always find the good and beauty in everyone. This gift will see you through the hard times."

I did not fully understand what she meant then, but her words would ring true as my life unfolded in the years ahead.

Over the years, Maria would have a profound influence on me, and it all started that one wintry day. We spent many days together either in her parlor or on her front porch. I was always at ease with her. She did not seem old, and she was truly interested in me, listening to every word without judgment. She had many stories of her own life that would prove to be lessons for me in the future. This special friendship would last through some very difficult times that yet lay ahead. Maria's strength, love, and wisdom would help me immensely.

Swedish people have a reputation for being stoic. They tend not to show their emotions very much, and conversations are rarely about personal concerns. Maria filled a void in my life when I needed to talk about matters I could not discuss with Mother or anyone else. For instance, when I became curious about some of the warm and exciting feelings I experienced at various times. Or when I would awaken from a dream about a boy and have strange yet nice sensations.

One day, after a few minutes of enjoying our tea, I dared to ask, "Maria, I do not know whom else to talk to, but I am having such strange dreams and sensations." I went on to explain some of the dreams and how my body and mind responded to them.

"My goodness, young lady! You certainly know how to come right to the point, don't you?" Her sweet laughter filled the air while we sat on the porch enjoying the warm spring weather. "Yes, I know what you're talking about. First of all, what you're experiencing is perfectly normal."

I quickly responded, "Oh, I am so glad to hear you say that! Do you mind if I ask some very personal questions?" I was feeling quite embarrassed and unsure if I should continue. I just knew I could not talk to Ingrid or Mother.

Thus began a long conversation about the beauty and functions of the male and female bodies, the magic of childbirth, and the importance of love.

She explained, "My child, do not be afraid of the changes your body is experiencing and the emotions attached to them. You're becoming a woman—and a beautiful one at that. Someday when you fall in love, marry, and have children, then all these physical feelings will be acted upon."

"Were you ever in love and married?" I asked.

She shared how she had fallen in love with James Johnson, her childhood sweetheart. They had grown up in Hoboken, where both their families farmed. She and James attended the one-room schoolhouse and the same Lutheran church.

"It seemed we always knew we were meant to be together. We were best friends. We spent every moment together. Therefore, it was only natural that we married as soon as James finished school. He was two years older than me, so I never finished school. The only thing I wanted was to be with him."

A smile went across her face as she looked off in the distance, recalling her wedding day.

"That day, we made a commitment to always love each other and be together. We planned to raise a family and live to an old age right here." She gestured to the home around her. "Only, we had a little less than ten years together before the war began and James joined the Union army. He had volunteered to serve for something we both believed was right for our country. He died valiantly at the Battle of Gettysburg in July 1863."

I learned that Maria and her husband started the Whispering Pines Inn shortly after marrying in 1851, providing comfortable beds, large rooms, and a restaurant, where Maria did the cooking and serving. They both were well liked and respected. James had been elected mayor and was bringing about many new changes to the then-small town when he left to fight the Confederates.

Maria continued to successfully run the hotel, always waiting for James to come home so they could live their lives together as they planned.

"Then one day I got a telegram that James had been killed."

Maria became quiet, lowered her eyes to her hands, and gently began to stroke her gold wedding ring.

A moment later, she deeply sighed. "I know he's waiting for me—I will join him when God says it's time for me to go home to him. I still love him as much as ever." She leaned over and patted my hand. "You see, Albertina, true love never dies but lives forever. I talk to him all the time. I believe he can hear me. In some unexplained way, I know he talks to me through my dreams, moments of inspiration, or times of quiet when unexpected memories or thoughts come into my mind." Maria looked at me and laughed. "Do I sound a little crazy to you?"

"Oh no—not at all. Everything you said is so beautiful. I hope someday I will find that same kind of love."

"You will, my child, if you let your heart guide you and if you listen to only it. Do not listen to other people or let your fears stop you. Unconditional true love is a gift from God, and few of us are patient or heartwise enough to wait for it or accept it when it's given."

The months of January and February 1879 brought many snow-storms and cold temperatures. At times, the road from the farm was impassable, requiring Mother to stay overnight at the inn. I was now in the twelfth grade, and I often missed school during those months. Whenever I was away from the classroom, I tried to imagine what my life would be like after graduation. Would I marry and have children? Would I always work as a cook at the inn, just as Mother did? I prayed I would find my purpose in life and live it to the fullest.

No matter how deep the snow, I always made my way through drifts and hills to spend a little time among the snow-laden trees. There was a special magic to the forest on those days, as if snow fairies were darting from tree to tree, spreading angel dust and whispering secrets. I felt Papa's presence, and I knew that in some mysterious way he was with me.

I had learned from Papa that every creature, plant, or tree has a special purpose or role, just as each of us humans have a reason to be here. We are the guardians of the land and animals, yet they are here also to fill our needs for food, protection, and beauty.

"Albertina, have you ever wondered why there are so many different kinds of animals?" Papa once asked after we had returned from a walk in the woods.

I was sitting on a stool by his feet. I looked up at him, shook my head, and listened intently as he went on.

"Just as each human is uniquely different, each animal has its purpose to provide food for us and other animals. But how dull life would be if the only animals we had were just bears, for instance. All we would see were bears—no birds, butterflies, cats or dogs, squirrels, or even spiders."

"I wish there were no spiders," I interrupted. "They scare me, and they are ugly."

"But spiders eat gnats, flies, and other pesky creatures. Again, each animal or plant has a purpose, in the same way you or I do."

"What is my purpose, Papa?"

Papa patted his knee for me to sit upon it. He wrapped his arm around me, and I leaned against his strong and broad chest.

In a soft and tender voice he assured me. "Someday you will discover what your purpose is. I know my purpose here is to be a good father and husband, to teach you as much as I can about life, and to provide food and shelter for you and your mother." He took a long puff of his pipe and added, "Love is the key to everything in life. Without love, there is nothing."

Though it had been many years since Papa and I had had this conversation, I still could hear his words. As I stood under the trees covered with snow, I asked myself, "How will I know what my purpose is? Will I recognize it? I pray that it will be clearly revealed to me."

In Sweden, every Sunday our family went to the Lutheran church, then spent a quiet afternoon at home. We followed the tradition of having a large meal in the afternoon followed by a day of rest. Papa always made sure to be home and did only the necessary chores, such as tending to the animals. We would play checkers or read, or I would play with the Dalecarlian horse Papa made. I made up stories in my mind about my Dalecarlian horse and me. It was a special family time.

In church, the sermons were mainly about the evil of sin, the downfall of man, and the need for repentance. Sometimes I was frightened as Pastor Swenson raised his right arm, sweeping it across the congregation, pointing and shaking his index finger at what seemed to be just me! I would curl my arm into my papa's strong arm and lean my head against him. With his other hand, he would pat my head, reassuring me that all was okay. I was always relieved when the organ would strike up its music so I could stand and sing. The scarier the sermon, the louder I sang.

When I was about eight years old, I asked Papa and Mother how God could let his only Son die. I did not understand how this could be a loving thing to do. They both agreed that it was hard to understand.

"We could not let anything ever happen to you, because we love you," Mother said. "That is why we marvel about God's love. God loves each of us so much, He sacrificed his only Son for us. God is beyond our full understanding, yet we know He is our Creator, Protector, and Guide." She then looked deeply into my eyes and said, "Someday all this will make more sense to you, then you too will know the Truth."

Here in Hoboken, I quietly walked through the woods and thought about the church's teachings, Papa's beliefs in woodland beings, and Mother's words about God. I tried to sort out how the beliefs agreed or supported one another.

In Sweden, there were only Lutheran churches, while in America, there were Methodist, Catholic, and Episcopalian churches in addition to Lutheran. The churches had some similar beliefs but also some distinctly different ones.

And our pastor in Sweden taught us the traditional Biblical teachings without dismissing the power of the mythical elves and älvas. But here in America, there was no such recognition or discussion. The only time I heard anyone talk about an elf, saw a ceramic gnome in a garden, or listened to a mythical tale of the forest was when I was in the presence of other Swedish immigrants.

Nels and Ingrid shared a few stories with me. A favorite story Ingrid told me was about a gnome.

"Did you know that some gnomes help farmers take care of their livestock and land?"

I nodded. "Mother has told me a little bit about the gnomes."

"Well, Grandma Hallgren believed in gnomes and used to see tiny footprints in the snow or soil around the farm buildings. She and Grandpa believed that one such gnome helped them with small chores during the night."

Aunt Ingrid smiled at me and said, "But you are now in America, Albertina. You must learn to adapt to the American way. Many people might think you are crazy if you tell them about your beliefs in elves, gnomes, and älvas."

CHAPTER 4

CHRISTMAS MEETING

1881

Christmas of 1881 was filled with excitement. We observed the traditions we brought with us from Sweden.

The tradition of the magic walnuts was very special to me because it had been handed down from Papa's family. Every Christmas morning back in Sweden, Mother and I would find walnut shells hanging from the tree, one for each of us. Each was hung from colorful ribbon with our name written on it. Once we opened our shells, we each found a folded piece of paper with a message of love from Papa. I saved every note and kept them in a small wooden box Papa had made for me.

I was glad to learn that the Lutheran church here in Hoboken celebrated the Festival of Saint Lucia every year on December 13. It was such an important part of the Christmas season in Sweden. According to Swedish legend, a ship arrived on the shore of our largest lake, Lake Värmland. Aboard was a young woman clothed in white and a crown of lit candles on her head. She distributed food and clothing to the needy during a great famine. Since then, young women have represented this saint in church services, wearing crowns of lighted candles, bringing light to the longest night of the year. Often the eldest daughter dresses in a white gown with a red sash and brings a tray of hot coffee and buns to her sleeping parents. It is a custom I still observed, bringing my tray of goodies to Mother, Ingrid, and Nels.

On Christmas Eve, we went to the church service. Lighted candles filled the sanctuary. At the close of the service, we each held a candle while singing "Silent Night." Once home, we enjoyed traditional meatballs, mashed potatoes, squash, and bread, all of which Ingrid and Mother prepared. I helped by rolling the meatballs and peeling the potatoes, trying to follow all the instructions they each gave me. Over the years, I had learned how to prepare many recipes and had developed skills as a rather accomplished cook. Mrs. Johnson was happy to hire me as second cook at the inn. However, Mother and Ingrid were the main cooks for special occasions.

The two sisters laughed and cried recalling past memories of family, friends, and each other as young girls. They shared stories of their lives and memories. I knew their stories were important lessons for me, even though some were painful for Mother and Ingrid.

They were the only children, two years apart and always the best of friends despite their differences. Ingrid was shy, quiet, a caregiver to many, and less interested in school and world events; whereas Mother loved school and was always asking questions, trying to understand why different countries, including Sweden, invaded and conquered other countries.

"Why can we not just live side by side in peace?" she would ask. "We do not need more land, nor must we all be the same. I think it is wonderful that there are people who look different than us and have different beliefs and cultures. It makes the world a beautiful kaleidoscope." But Mother's words went on deaf ears. Most people did not care about anything, except what was happening in their own family. Too often they sent their sons into battle without questioning the government or army.

I learned more about my grandparents, aunt, and mother while I sat in on their conversations that Christmas Eve. My grandfather Hallgren was the eldest son and took over the family farm. He was slender of build but made up for it with his muscular strength and strong determination. He was gentle and sweet to his wife, my grandmother, yet strict with his two daughters, not afraid to discipline them with spankings.

"I always thought he treated us as if we were the sons he never had," Mother said. "I know he loved us, and he was very good to us. He taught us to be strong and independent, while most girls were raised to be dependent and submissive to their husbands."

Ingrid wrapped a curl around her finger and almost whispered, "I really loved Father, but I also had a certain fear of him. I did not want to disappoint him." After a few minutes, she continued, "If I had a child, I would want Nels to be the same kind of father to our son or daughter." Then as if waking up from a dreamy state, she said, "Well, I have not been blessed with a child, and I suppose by this age, I won't be. I wonder why each of us have had so much trouble having a child."

I listened to the two sisters exchange stories about their desires and struggles to have children. I was considered the wonder child, a true gift from God, so Mother and Father chose the name Albertina Angela. The first name was for my grandfather, Albert Hallgren, and Angela was for all the guardian angels that watched over Mother throughout her difficult pregnancy.

"I am so blessed to have Albertina," Mother said as if she were unaware of my presence, even though I was sitting right by her. "I treasure every moment with her, and I want to teach her everything so she will have a safe, fulfilled, and loving life. I hope she will someday have the same kind of love for a man that I have for my dear Gustaf." Mother wiped some tears with her embroidered handkerchief and kept repeating, "I miss him so much."

Both sisters had fallen in love with their partners for life and continued that love even after death. One lost her husband too soon, while the other lost all her children before they were able to begin life. Even at such a young age, just entering adulthood, I prayed I would also receive the gift of unconditional love for a husband and have children.

Ingrid's employers, Mr. and Mrs. Saint-Gaudens, planned an open house for December 20 for those who worked at their studios and home. Ingrid prepared most of the food for the special day, eliciting help from Mother. She not only prepared her famous meatballs, cabbage, and various desserts but also raw oysters, roasted turkey, quail, yams, potatoes, and a variety of Swedish cookies. Mrs. Saint-Gaudens hired outside help to attend to the buffet the night of the party, which allowed Ingrid to enjoy the evening. Ingrid and Nels were quite adamant that Mother and I should also attend.

Mother said, "I do not belong there among so many people who speak English so well. And besides, neither Albertina nor I have a dress pretty enough to wear."

"Do not be foolish, my dear sister. You both speak the language beautifully. Really, all you have to do is smile and listen. Most people just want to hear themselves talk," Ingrid coaxed Mother. "And the dresses you wear to church are fine. I will comb your hair in a stylish way and put pretty ribbons in it."

Mother was a proud woman who always wanted to present herself in a way that showed her strengths, independence, and ability to handle any situation. Since arriving in America, she used every opportunity at the inn to practice her English, and she read books out loud each evening. She put every spare cent away in a small account at the local bank. She preached to me three important creeds by which to live: One, frugality is important, yet so is generosity to those in need. Two, it is not the clothing, jewels, or fancy things of the world that make a person great, but rather love and kindness. And three, honest work gives a person both a strong back and strong character.

Mother was shy around new people, especially since leaving Sweden. She was in the kitchen at the inn cooking all day, so she was not used to being around many people. But she reluctantly agreed to go to the party once Ingrid assured her she would enjoy being with the other people.

The home of Mr. and Mrs. Saint-Gaudens was a two-story brownstone at 22 Washington Place. The porch was decorated with balsam garland and red ribbons. Two small pine trees graced each side of the majestic front door, welcoming us while we timidly stepped into the large foray. The house was filled with the many people who worked at the studio as well as at their home.

I stood close to my mother while I took in all the splendor, music, and gaiety that filled this magnificent house, which was the largest I had ever been in. Servants offered glasses of champagne, and many platters and bowls of food were beautifully spread out on a large table.

"There is enough food here to feed us for a year," I blurted out as I filled my plate to almost overflowing.

"Albertina, do not be a little pig. Remember you are a young lady, not a pig." Mother placed only a couple of small portions on her plate.

"Madam, there is plenty of food. What you have there would not fill the tiniest of birds."

We turned to see a distinguished middle-aged gentleman standing next to us. He was dressed in a tuxedo with a black bow tie crookedly lying under his nicely trimmed red beard. His thick hair was more golden than red. I could see a gold chain that obviously led to a gold watch in a hidden pocket.

"I do not believe we have met before, so let me introduce myself. I am Augustus Saint-Gaudens, and I welcome you to my home."

Mother gave a slight bow and introduced both of us. He bowed and lightly kissed our hands.

He was of medium build and short of stature—only slightly taller than Mother. His hazel eyes were lively, drawing me into his gaze. When his lips curved up into a smile, they revealed the whitest of teeth. I half giggled to myself, thinking, "He must paint his teeth for them to be so white!" I lowered my eyes, and with my handkerchief over my mouth, I turned partly away, hoping my secret little joke would not be suspected.

I was surprised when he unexpectedly took my chin in his hand and turned my head back toward him and then in different positions.

"You have a beautiful head and exquisite beauty. I should like to do a sketch of you someday." He spoke with an accent, and I could not quite decide from where it came. In time, I would learn it was a mixture of Irish, French, and English.

"I do not think that will be possible," Mother said crisply. "It was nice to meet you, Mr. Saint-Gaudens. Thank you for the wonderful party," she added.

Before I realized what was happening, Mother took my hand and led me away, out the door. I was frightened. I thought Mother had somehow read my mind and knew my secret joke about our host's teeth. Or had I said or done something to upset her?

Once we were outside and away from the house, I asked, "Mother, what is wrong?"

"My dear child, you are so young and innocent—you do not know that sometimes people have unkind intentions." Mother seemed to quicken her step once we reached Nels's wagon to carry us back to the farm.

"I don't understand. What did I do?"

"You did nothing wrong. You were a perfect little lady." She paused before she continued, "I am sure Mr. Saint-Gaudens did not mean anything unkind by asking to do some sketches of you, but you are a child. It was most improper for him to touch you and then talk about your beauty."

Nels soon joined us and was quite surprised that Mother was ready to go home.

"But we just got here. We have not eaten or danced," Nels complained. "Please, let us go back and enjoy the evening. For Ingrid's sake, we cannot insult or upset Mr. and Mrs. Saint-Gaudens by leaving so quickly and without any apparent reason."

Mother reluctantly agreed, but she made sure Mr. Saint-Gaudens was always on the other side of the room from us. Mother's grim face made me most uncomfortable and confused. How could she not smile and enjoy the music? I was tapping my foot and so wanting to dance, but I graciously declined each invitation.

We returned to the farm without any exchange of words from

anyone, riding in silence down to the port and then boarding the ferry. We entered through the farmhouse back door and stood in the kitchen as we removed our wraps and scarves.

"Mother, I am not a child anymore," I finally said. "I will be twenty years old on my next birthday. I am a young adult and older than you were when you and Papa married."

Mother looked deeply into my eyes. She smiled while tears began to fill her eyes. One tear trickled down her rosy-red cheek. Just as I reached up to dry her tear, she wrapped me in her arms.

"Oh, my sweet little Albertina. You are a young woman and so beautiful. Mr. Saint-Gaudens was correct when he said you have exquisite beauty."

We stood there for a few minutes, rocking back and forth in time to music only the two of us heard.

"My daughter is growing up and has become a beautiful woman right before my eyes. Yet I still think of you as my little girl who needs a mother's protection. Just know that my actions are out of love for you."

That night in bed, my mind swirled with thoughts, dreams, and emotions I could not share with Mother. She was obviously unsure about Mr. Saint-Gaudens's boldness. However, I knew I could always talk to Maria.

CHAPTER 5

THE STUDIO

1882

I remember it was early March when I saw Mr. Saint-Gaudens again. I had not seen him since the Christmas party. Ingrid had told us about the many wonderful art pieces he was doing; the recognition he had received for his sculpture, *Hiawatha;* and his work on *Farragut Monument.* He had traveled to Paris and Italy, then back to New York. In fact, Mr. and Mrs. Saint-Gaudens had recently returned from Paris after living there for three years.

I was walking toward town to begin my work at the inn. Rather than trek through the wet mud on the road, I chose to make my way on the icy sludge on the side. I heard hoofbeats coming up behind me, and I quickly glanced back at the approaching black carriage. It went by me so quickly that mud splattered all over my coat.

The carriage suddenly stopped. The door opened, and to my surprise, Mr. Saint-Gaudens carefully stepped out and made his way to me.

"I am so sorry, miss. My driver was going too fast, hoping to not get stuck in the muddy ruts."

I recognized him right away and curtsied. "I am all right."

For an awkward time, we just stood there. I was not afraid or uncomfortable, though I kept my eyes cast down, as I was taught to do.

"Look at me, for I do believe you are the very young lady I came here looking for." He put my hood down, held my chin, and in a quiet voice—almost a whisper—said, "I never forget a beautiful face, and you my dear one, are such a beauty."

I could feel a rush of blood fill my cheeks. My whole body felt hot, though the air was cold. I stepped back. His hand fell to his side, and when I peered up, his hazel eyes were gazing deeply into mine.

I again curtsied and stammered, "I—I—I must go now, sir. It was nice to see you again."

I grabbed the folds of my coat, turned, and started to walk toward the inn. My feet slipped on the half-frozen ground, but my rubbery legs somehow kept me erect. I began to shiver from the cold. Or was I just excited to see him?

"Wait!" he called out after me. "Please come to my studio tomorrow. I would like to do some preliminary sketches." He came walking up beside me. "I have traveled all the way from New York City to see you. I will not take no for an answer."

I shook my head. "I am sorry, sir. I do not think I can. My mother would not approve."

He smiled and nodded. "I do not mean to be rude, but Albertina, I must talk to you and your mother. Today is as good as any other. Is it not?"

He had a twinkle in his eyes, and his smile was contagious. He tipped his hat and motioned to his carriage.

"Now please get in, and let's go talk to your mother. Besides, you are so cold."

I hesitated, but he kept insisting, and the coldness of the air was penetrating deeply. I finally got in and sat down on the carriage seat. He quickly placed one blanket around my shoulders and another on my lap.

"Thank you, sir. You are most kind."

"Now let us go talk to your mother."

"Oh, sir, she is working at the inn now. We cannot disturb her. She is very conscientious about doing her job correctly and giving Mrs. Johnson all the time for which she is paid."

It was the truth. But I also knew Mother would be quite upset if I showed up at the Whispering Pines Inn with Mr. Saint-Gaudens, especially if she knew I had been in his carriage.

Still not taking no for an answer, he instructed the driver to go to the inn.

As I suspected, Mother was not happy as I entered the inn's kitchen with Mr. Saint-Gaudens at my side. Her stern look stopped me from going any closer, but Mr. Saint-Gaudens continued to approach Mother.

"My dear Mrs. Hultgren, how nice to see you again. In case you do not remember, I am Augustus Saint-Gaudens. We met a few months ago at the Christmas party in my home."

Mother's eyes shifted from him to me, trying to comprehend why her young daughter would not only interrupt her work but also be in the company of someone she considered being a rude and flirtatious artist.

Rather coldly, Mother replied, "I remember you. Might I ask what you are doing here with my daughter? I have a job to do. I cannot waste my employer's time."

Mr. Saint-Gaudens nodded graciously. "I quite understand. If there is any problem, I will personally talk to Mrs. Johnson, who is a friend of mine." He turned and pointed back at me. "Since I first saw your daughter last Christmas, I have envisioned using her as a model for a sculpture I am planning to do. However, I need to first do some sketches of her to determine how I might want her to pose. I—"

Before he could continue, Mother interrupted him. "My daughter will *not* be doing any posing for you, Mr. Saint-Gaudens. Now if you will excuse us, my daughter and I have work to do."

She looked back toward me. I immediately went to her side. Mother took my hand, said "Good day, sir," turned on her heel, and walked us to the stove, where she turned her attention to the bubbling pot of soup.

For the rest of the afternoon and early evening, Mother and I exchanged no words. I helped prepare the meal, set tables, and do the dishes while hiding my feelings and tears. I was enchanted by Mr. Saint-Gaudens. I wanted him to do the sketches. I wanted to be with him.

Once home, I went straight to my room. I felt too flushed, excited, and confused to talk to anyone. For the longest time, I just sat on the edge of my bed, reliving every minute with Mr. Saint-Gaudens. I felt hot, then suddenly cold, then hot again. "Am I sick?" I asked myself, trying to understand these physical sensations.

"He said I was beautiful," I told myself. I gazed at my reflection in the mirror, turning my head side to side. I did not see beauty. I saw two large and round eyes, a long nose, and cheekbones that seemed chiseled on too small a face.

"I am not a beauty. I am just plain me."

Suddenly I felt quite tired, so I stretched out on the bed. I threw a quilt over me, closed my eyes, and drifted off to sleep, thinking, "I must talk to Maria."

The following Sunday afternoon while I was in the kitchen, I heard Uncle Nels answer the front door.

"Good day, Mr. Saint-Gaudens. Please come in."

I peeked around the corner and felt my knees go weak. There was Mr. Saint-Gaudens standing in the parlor. His red hair seemed to brighten up the room.

"I apologize for coming unannounced, but I would like to talk to Mrs. Hultgren."

"Yes, of course. Please have a seat. I will tell her you are here." Uncle Nels shuffled backward and nervously said, "I think she is out in the chicken barn, gathering some eggs. Just make yourself comfortable, sir."

He turned and almost bumped into me as he entered the kitchen. He whispered, "He wants to see your mother. Why do you suppose?"

I bit my lower lip and shook my head.

As Uncle Nels left to find Mother, I paced around the kitchen, wiping my hands on my apron. I tried to imagine what possible reason Mr. Saint-Gaudens would be here. I relived our meeting on the road. I did not do anything wrong. I was polite. I backed away when his hand touched my face. But had I not backed away quickly enough? Did he think I had been flirting with him? Was that why he was here? I also relived his discussion with Mother. Had she not been as clear to him as she had been to me?

Mother entered the kitchen and quickly glanced at me with what appeared to be a question on her face. I am sure she was also surprised that Mr. Saint-Gaudens had come uninvited. She set down the basket of eggs and swept her hands over her bodice and skirt, brushing away any strands of straw. Then she tucked a few wisps of hair behind her ears. Straightening her back and shoulders, she held her head erect and walked into the parlor.

"How nice to see you, Mr. Saint-Gaudens. May I offer you some tea?" Before he could respond, she called into the kitchen, "Albertina, please bring some tea and cookies into the parlor."

I did not want to go in there and see him. I was scared I had done something wrong, though I could not think of any action that could have possibly been considered disrespectful or unkind. In panic, I grabbed my coat and opened the back door, hoping to escape to the nearby woods. There I could reminisce about my two encounters with Mr. Saint-Gaudens and determine why he would be at my aunt and uncle's house asking to see my mother.

"Where are you going, child?" Uncle Nels whispered. "Did you not hear your mother ask for some tea and cookies to be brought into the parlor?"

I closed the partially opened door and muttered, "Yes, sir."

I hung my coat back up on its familiar brass hook and proceeded to arrange some cookies on the oval pewter tray. I filled the matching pewter teapot with hot water and a teabag. I completed the tray with cups and saucers, a sugar bowl, creamer, spoons, and napkins. I was sure our simple wares did not compare to the fine silver pieces he was accustomed to, but right then, I did not particularly care.

Upon my entering the room, he arose from his chair. "Good morning, miss." With a slight bow, he added, "It is nice to see you again."

My hands were shaking so much that the cups and dishes rattled. "Here—let me take the tray for you."

I felt my cheeks begin to burn, and my whole body suddenly felt hot. I turned to leave the room.

"Please stay," he said. "I would like to talk to both you and your mother."

I shuddered, faintly nodded my head, and sat on the sofa next to Mother, who had a surprised and confused expression on her face.

When Mother and I looked at each other ever so briefly, I saw a hint of fear in her eyes. What was she thinking? Was she thinking back to when Mr. Saint-Gaudens and I appeared at the inn unexpectedly?

At first, Mr. Saint-Gaudens led some polite small talk about the weather, the state of the economy, and some local gossip. Then he cleared his throat.

After a short pause, he said, "Mrs. Hultgren, the first time I met you and your daughter at our Christmas party, I told you I was quite impressed with her beauty. As I have said before, she has a very noble head with such fine features. I would like to do some sketches of her and possibly have her pose for a sculpture I am planning to do—of course, with your permission and complete supervision."

He paused again briefly and sat forward in his seat. "I do apologize for barging in on you at the inn last week. It was very rude and thought-less on my part. It is just that I know your daughter has the perfect face for my sculpture."

Mother looked over at me, then at our guest, and then to me. "I do appreciate the kind and flattering things you have said about Albertina, but I just could not permit such a thing." Mother ran her long delicate fingers along the creases of her skirt.

"I can assure you, madam, that my intentions are most honorable. As an artist, I know beauty when I see it, and your daughter is just such a beauty. I have been asked by Cornelius Vanderbilt to design a mantel-piece for the entry hall of his estate. My vision is of two angelic figures supporting the piece." He took a sip of his tea and watched my mother's reaction. "Mr. Vanderbilt is a very successful businessman, and I am so honored to have this opportunity."

Then quite unexpectedly, he looked at me. I had been looking at him with my mouth slightly agape, surprised to hear such flattering words spoken of me.

He briefly paused, then looked back toward Mother. "Mrs. Hultgren, perhaps you and your daughter might come to my studio, meet my wife and brother, and let me show you some samples of my work. Your sister works at our home and also occasionally brings food to my studio. You can be sure your daughter would be safe. Besides, my wife frequently comes to the studio."

After a moment of silence, Mother stood up and walked to the window facing west toward the nearby woods. The stillness of the room was heavy and thick. I felt faint and took a sip of tea, hoping it would strengthen me.

Mother turned toward us and spoke in almost a whisper. "Mr. Saint-Gaudens, once again, my daughter and I are flattered by your compliments. I have always thought she was a beautiful angel and have protected her from people who might take advantage of her." She sat down on the sofa next to me, put her arm around me, and said, "I will talk to Albertina, and we will send a message to you as to our decision."

She squeezed my shoulder, then arose and extended her hand to our guest. "Thank you for coming. We wish you a good day."

We stood side by side, watching Mr. Saint-Gaudens climb into his awaiting carriage. The cool air of that April day felt healing against my hot face.

"Daughter, we need to talk."

I told Mother I did feel safe with Mr. Saint-Gaudens, but that I was nervous about the situation. I was worried I would say or do something inappropriate or embarrassing. Plus, I was still having a hard time accepting Mr. Saint-Gaudens's flattery.

"Mother, *you* are the beauty in the family, and I don't just mean physically," I said. "You are so kind and gentle to everyone, and you have a beautiful face. I would think Mr. Saint-Gaudens would want to sketch you instead of me."

She smiled and said with a little laughter, "I am too old. My youthful features are gone." I tried to interrupt her, but she continued, "I want to be serious now: Beauty can be a gift or a curse. It depends on how you use it."

I returned her gaze.

"You must never take your beauty for granted, nor be ungrateful, nor use it to bring hurt or harm to others. Do you understand?"

I nodded, though I was not completely sure how my looks could cause anyone harm.

We agreed to visit Mr. Saint-Gaudens's studio the following week.

The Sherwood Studio Building was located at Sixth Avenue and Fifty-Seventh Street. Mr. Saint-Gaudens's studio space inside the building was small but filled with various pieces of plaster, mounds of scattered sheets of paper with drawings, and a few men who were working on smaller pieces. I gasped in awe and squeezed Mother's hand as I tried to take in all that was before me.

In the center of the room was a massive piece of white marble with ladders and scaffolding around it. Two men hammered against chisels, breaking off various sizes and shapes of the marble. Their work appeared haphazard to my uneducated eyes, but the man directing them appeared to have confidence in what they were doing. This man had the same stature of Mr. Saint-Gaudens, except his hair was a dark brown and he had no beard. There was a similar look and a nervous energy to his movements.

Suddenly, we heard Mr. Saint-Gaudens's voice saying, "You are watching my brother Louis, who is my right-hand man and an artist in his own right. Come—let me introduce you." He extended his left arm, inviting us to follow him.

As we neared, I could hear the brother's baritone voice shouting instructions: "Take a little more there" and "No, Samuel—strike the chisel firmly but gently" and "That is good, very good." He waved his arms over and around as if he were conducting an orchestra. I found it magical.

"Louis, my dear brother, stop your work for just a moment, please." Mr. Saint-Gaudens said these words with such love in his voice.

After introductions and some small talk, Mr. Saint-Gaudens went on, "This is the young lady I was telling you about, the one I would like to sketch. Do you agree she is perfect for the Vanderbilt project?"

The two brothers walked around me while never taking their eyes off me. They exchanged their impressions and thoughts sometimes in English, but mainly in French. I heard phrases such as "angular head," "high cheekbones," and "vibrant eyes."

I felt a mix of embarrassment and pride. My cheeks were warm, my heart beat fast, and my knees began to shake. I had never experienced such attention. Once again, I asked myself the same question: "Am I really pretty?"

I glanced over at Mother, who was watching and listening to the brothers, trying to understand their words and gestures.

Then I was suddenly brought out of my dreamlike state when I heard Mother say, "Come Albertina. It is time to go to work." She turned to the two artists and said, "Perhaps you will come to our home on Sunday at four o'clock in the afternoon to discuss your ideas for Albertina. I want my sister, Ingrid, and her husband to be a part of whatever decision we make. They have lived in this country long enough to have a good command of the English language. Besides, they are my only family, and I trust their judgment in all things."

Mr. Saint-Gaudens bowed and replied, "Of course, madam, I will be there. But before you leave, I would like you both to meet my wife and have some tea. Our home is just a short carriage ride from here."

Mother responded, "We met Mrs. Saint-Gaudens at the Christmas party, but the meeting was brief. We will be honored to meet her again. However, we will not be able to stay long. We have been away long enough, and we need to return to the inn. Time has by gone so rapidly."

Mrs. Saint-Gaudens was an austere woman whose features showed a permanent crease between her eyebrows even when she smiled. She was tall and large boned, with penetrating brown eyes and a deep dimple in her chin.

The year before, Mrs. Saint-Gaudens had given birth to a son. She proudly held him in her arms upon greeting us.

"This is my son, Homer."

She then quickly turned and handed the handsome little boy over to his nanny.

From her thin lips, she expressed her pleasure in meeting us, albeit stiffly. Perhaps that was her natural demeanor. But then again, perhaps she was not pleased at all. Her rather plain dark-gray dress was unadorned with any lace or jewelry, as would be expected of a woman of her economic status. I wondered if she were in mourning, though Ingrid had not shared about any death in the family.

Mrs. Saint-Gaudens and Mother exchanged pleasantries for a few minutes. During this time, I was well aware of how often Mrs. Saint-Gaudens looked at me. My impression was that she did not like me. Her eyes were cold and her words were harsh when she spoke.

CHAPTER 6

NEW CAREER

1882

The following evening after supper, Mother gathered us all in the parlor. We all agreed—even Mother—that we liked Mr. Saint-Gaudens and believed he was an honest, respectable gentleman with only the best intentions. Ingrid shared how pleasant and kind he always was to the staff and how he had a wonderful sense of humor. He liked to draw caricatures and cartoons, she said.

"His brother Louis is also a good man," Ingrid added. "He's so quiet and well mannered, sometimes you almost forget he is even in the room. He comes and goes almost unseen between the studio and house." She paused and looked down at her hands before saying in a most quiet voice, "Just between us, I don't think Louis likes Mrs. Saint-Gaudens. I have never heard them even exchange a greeting in the morning." Then she glanced up at us and said, "I shouldn't be passing on gossip. Just forget what I said."

Mother sipped her tea and nibbled at a cookie, listening to everyone's comments and thoughts. After a while, she said, "I certainly trust the opinion of my own sister, who has great respect and admiration for both Mr. Saint-Gaudens and his brother."

She paused and picked some crumbs off her skirt and delicately dropped them onto the tea saucer.

"I also talked to my employer, Mrs. Johnson, who also had very kind things to say about both of the brothers. She did say Mrs. Saint-Gaudens is rather gruff and can appear to be quite rude, mainly due to her inability to hear well. But she travels a lot, and Albertina will probably not be in her presence very often."

She looked at me and reached over to stroke my cheek.

"I will agree for you to do this posing, but there will be certain requests I will insist upon with Mr. Saint-Gaudens."

After our discussion that day, Mother met with Mr. Saint-Gaudens to discuss her decision. I never knew the full details of their agreement.

"You are but a child who does not need to fill her head with business," Mother told me. "All you need to know is that you will go to the studio every day with Ingrid, except Sundays."

Mother put her arms around my waist and nestled her nose into my hair.

"You are so beautiful, and it is your beauty that will bring some extra money into our home. Your papa would be so proud of you."

She then stepped away from me, turned toward the window, and took her handkerchief to her face. I knew she was thinking of Papa.

Many thoughts began to run through my mind. "Here I am, twenty years old, working as a cook. Will working for Mr. Saint-Gaudens be the start of a new life? Will I be happy? What is it really like to pose for an artist?"

But then I could feel my chest tighten as I realized I was taking a big step out into the world. "Am I doing the right thing? Am I thinking with emotion and not my mind? What if I let Mr. Saint-Gaudens and my family down?"

Suddenly, the walls seemed to be closing in around me. I ran out of the house. I was hot, yet a chill ran through my body, like the ice floes from the waters of the Arctic Ocean.

Once I threw open the door and stepped out into the spring

sunshine, I felt a calm and peace. I made my way to the nearby woods and sighed with happiness to be there. I brushed my hand across each tree's rough bark. I felt the cool moisture of last autumn's fallen leaves beneath my shoes. And I breathed in the intoxicating smells of lilacs, pine, and apple and cherry blossoms. Once I could no longer see the farmhouse, I sat upon a large granite boulder and let all my senses take in the wonder of my surroundings.

"No wonder Papa loved the forests. They are so peaceful and beautiful," I whispered to myself, not wanting to disrupt the sounds of the wind whistling through the branches or the distant calls of blackbirds.

After several minutes of just listening to nature's sounds, I cried out loud, "Oh, Papa, I wish you were here! I am having so many different feelings, and I cannot talk about them with Mother."

I looked around, half of me expecting Papa to appear and the other half of me fearful some stranger had heard me.

"How foolish I am!" I thought. "I am in the woods talking to, what? Nothing but trees and birds."

I stood up and brushed my skirt. Suddenly I saw something out of the corner of my eye. But when I looked closely, nothing was there except a very old and tall pine tree. The tree's limbs stretched out far and wide, making it the center around which smaller pine trees stood.

Just as I turned to leave, a voice said, "Child, you are not alone."

I looked back toward the old pine tree and could see a glow of light coming from behind its massive trunk. The blue-green rays of light shimmered and danced.

"I am an älva," the voice said. "I am always with you in the forest, to protect and guide you."

I felt safe, completely in awe of the brilliant, yet not harsh, light that warmed and comforted me. The älva's words were not spoken in the traditional sense, but I could still hear and understand them. It was just the kind of experience Papa had talked about when he was in the woods.

"Do you know my papa?" I asked.

"Your papa is well known to all of us. We were often with him to protect and guide him." Then the light became gray, and sadness filled the forest. "We tried to warn him about the other tree, which we knew would fall where he was standing. He was working very hard and fast, trying to get as much work done before the sun set. He did not hear us. He was too distracted."

The light went dark. With tears streaming down my face, I slowly took steps toward where the light had been.

"Please do not leave. Please come back."

I stretched my arm out, gently touching the old tree's trunk, running my fingers along the rough edges. I slowly lowered myself against the base, leaned my head against it, wiped away the tears, and looked up at the shafts of sunlight filtering through its outstretched limbs.

"Please come back."

I must have fallen asleep, for suddenly I was aware of soreness in my back and buttocks. I blinked and looked around until I saw the large boulder I had earlier sat on. Once again I heard the caws of the black-birds and could smell spring's blossoms.

I stood and stepped back to look at the tree against which I had been leaning. I rubbed my eyes and looked again. The pine tree was just an ordinary one—no larger or majestic than any other tree. And there was neither a brilliant light nor particular darkness around it.

"Was I dreaming?" I asked myself. "Was this the only way Papa could talk to me?"

The next day, I walked into town to see Maria. I knew she would listen and give me good advice.

When I arrived at her house, she was on her knees in front of a flowerbed, busily churning the rich soil with a small hand claw, removing loose stones, and mixing dead leaves. For a brief moment, I just stood and watched her, admiring her ability to turn an early-spring garden filled with the autumn's and winter's debris into something clean and neat. Little crocuses with their purple-and-yellow tops had lifted their heads toward the sun, bringing color and beauty. They were the intro-duction of what was to come. In a few weeks, Maria would be planting her favorite red geraniums and impatiens among the hostas, large white chrysanthemums, and two lilac bushes. On each corner of the house stood two Japanese yews, tall and stately, like guards.

"Good morning, Maria," I said gently, trying not to startle her.

Nevertheless, she jumped and turned her head toward me. She raised her hand up to shield the sun.

"Oh, aren't you a sight for sore eyes! You look like an angel with the sun's beams radiating behind you." She got up with little groans and swept her hands down her skirt. "Oh, you'll have to forgive me for being so dirty and messy."

I laughed. "Oh, Maria, you look just as wonderful as always, even with this big smudge of dirt on your cheek." I took my kerchief and wiped her rosy cheek.

"Come—let's sit on the porch."

While we walked up the white creaking steps, Maria wiped her hands on her skirt again, trying to remove some dirt. Once seated, we just looked at each other for a minute, taking in the joy of being together, especially on such a glorious day.

"This is such a nice surprise to see you on a Monday. Don't you work at the inn today? Is everything all right?" She suddenly put one hand to her mouth, and the other she shook in the air. "Oh, forgive me. I'm asking too many questions!" Then she lowered her voice, and with her hands now in her lap, she declared, "I'm just a little excited because I'm so glad to see you."

I reached over and touched her folded hands. "I am glad to be here. A lot has happened recently, and I hope you don't mind if I ask for your advice."

Maria nodded and smiled.

I continued to tell her about Mr. Saint-Gaudens and his offer for me to pose, working for him every day and not returning to work at the inn.

"I am excited and nervous—I want to do what is right and be helpful for my family."

I paused and searched Maria's face for some reaction. As always, she had a sweet smile on her face and her gentle eyes met mine. I felt encouraged to share my feelings of excitement, some fear, and also concerns if I was making the right decision.

"When I was in his studio, it was like entering another world, and I did not want to leave it. I have never felt that way except when in the forest."

Maria asked me many questions, such as, "How will you feel being in this studio filled only with men?" and "Do you think you'll be able to sit or stand without moving for varying lengths of time?"

"I have known Mr. and Mrs. Saint-Gaudens for several years," she said. "He has always been most charming and kind. However, she has a reputation of being rude or unfriendly, which I have witnessed several times. She is quite hard of hearing, so this contributes to her problem of communicating with people."

And then Maria looked right at me and asked, "How do you feel about being around Gussie, Mrs. Saint-Gaudens?"

I could feel myself squirming in my chair, suddenly uncomfortable with the prospect.

"Do you think she will be there very often?" I asked.

Maria smiled knowingly. "No, I don't think so. Not very often. But there will be times when you will see each other." She patted my hand and said, "Gussie comes from a well-to-do family, and sometimes her demeanor reflects that. But don't worry about her. Just be you. Her bark is worse than her bite, my dear. Don't let her intimidate or frighten you."

Maria fell quiet for a minute and searched my eyes.

"Oh, my dear, it sounds to me like you're doing the right thing. I know your papa would be very proud of you." She stood, and the old rocking chair swung back and forth. "Come, child. Let's go in the kitchen for some coffee and cake. Let's celebrate this new chapter of your life."

CHAPTER 7

THE MODEL

1882

The next day, Ingrid and I went into New York City. She left me at Sherwood Studio Building, then went on to the home of the Saint-Gaudens.

"I will see you later, my dear. Just go on up."

I stood outside, took a deep breath, said a prayer, then slowly opened the door. The large room was relatively quiet with only two men standing on a scaffold and plank. Once my eyes adjusted to the light streaming in from the large windows, I recognized Louis standing at a large table, looking at sheets of paper, and mumbling inaudible words. I walked up and gently tapped him on the shoulder.

"Mr. Saint-Gaudens, it is I, Albertina Hultgren." My heart was pounding so hard I was fearful he could hear it.

Louis whirled around and stared at me as he tried to remember who I was. Then recognition filled his eyes, and he welcomed me with a wide grin.

"Oh, yes—Albertina! I was thinking so hard that I did not even hear you come in." He waved his hands over the papers with sketches and illegible words scrawled on them. "My brother has written these instructions for your first time here. I think I understand what he wants for today."

He ran his hand through his hair as he took my elbow and escorted me across the room. Once I had removed my bonnet and shawl, he had me sit on a high stool.

A little flustered and actually disappointed, I asked, "Is Mr. Saint-Gaudens not coming?"

"Oh, he will be in sometime soon. Now, just sit here quietly while I do some preliminary drawing."

Every now and then, he instructed me to turn my head this way or that, tilt my chin up or down, look to the left or right, and smile or pout. It was very tiring to hold some poses for what seemed a very long time.

Finally, I asked, "Sir, may I please take a rest? My neck is quite sore."

Still busy sketching, Louis did not answer right away. (He insisted I call him by his given name.) When I started to repeat my pleadings, he looked up with a smile and gave me permission to get up and stretch.

"I will make you a cup of tea, then we will start again."

I slowly sipped my cup of tea while taking in all the art, activity, and people in the small and well-lit room with wooden walls and high-beamed ceilings. The air seemed heavy with white dust. I watched the tiny particles dance like diamonds in the shafts of the sun's rays streaming through the eastern windows. I was enthralled. I became lost in the dance and drama of the activity, which Louis too quickly interrupted.

"Come, come—there are many more sketches to be done."

Instead of sitting on the stool, this time I was instructed to stand on a small platform.

More instructions came: "Turn to your left." "Now turn to your right." "Hold your arms out." And "Look at me across your shoulder with your back turned to me."

About an hour later, my legs began to shake from tiredness, and my back ached from holding it so straight and still. I began to feel nauseous from the headache that started in my right shoulder, traveled up my neck and across my skull, then spread into my right eye.

"Louis, I am sorry, but I must sit and rest," I said. "I think I am going to be sick."

Just as I took my first step down from the pedestal, the room began to spin. I fell to the floor in a faint.

I awoke to the sound of my name and the coolness of a damp cloth on my forehead. I was being held in the curvature of strong arms, and someone held my hand. Upon opening my eyes, I saw a golden beard and head of hair and hazel eyes gazing into mine.

Immediately, I was embarrassed. I tried to rise up out of his arms.

"Just rest, my child," Mr. Saint-Gaudens said in his kind and gentle voice. "You had a bit of a fall, and we want to make sure you are okay."

Enjoying the warmth and protection of his arms, I relaxed into his embrace, closed my eyes, and went in and out of a dreamlike state. I allowed my body to relax, though it felt as if a chisel and hammer were tapping on every muscle and nerve in my head.

I awakened once again to find myself on a velveteen chaise lounge. A multicolored quilt covered my tender body that was sore from the fall on my first day as a model. I sat up, straightened my clothes, and tucked the loosened long curls behind my ears.

Mr. Saint-Gaudens walked over. "How are you, my dear? I guess we worked you too hard on this, your first day." Again he took one of my hands in his. "You will come back tomorrow, yes? I have looked at the preliminary sketches, and I so want you to come back and be my model for the Vanderbilt mantelpiece."

I slowly nodded without looking into his eyes. I was so grateful and excited that he wanted me to return. I had been worried that I had failed.

"I will be back tomorrow morning, if you really want me to," I whispered.

I could feel his eyes on me, and I looked up when he said, "You are so beautiful and sweet. Of course I want you to come back tomorrow— and many mornings after that."

I felt relaxed, comfortable, and relieved in that he still wanted me at the studio. His kind mannerisms and reassurances brought a smile to my face.

At the time, the Vanderbilt name and the significance of this project meant nothing to me. I just wanted to be with Mr. Saint-Gaudens.

The days at the studio that followed were tiring, but I learned to be assertive in asking for tea breaks. Upon Louis's suggestion, I stretched my back, neck, and arms for a few seconds in between poses whenever I felt the muscles begin to tighten.

Over the weeks, I grew to appreciate the purpose of the many sketches and poses in preparation for the sculpture work. One afternoon, Mr. Saint-Gaudens was ready to begin his initial sculpting. He excitedly told me more about the mantelpiece for Cornelius Vanderbilt's mansion.

"I will take part in designing his fireplace. It will be large, measuring about fifteen feet long and eleven feet high. At each end of the piece will be an angelic figure. I can see them in my mind: one will represent Amor and the other Pax." His eyes were sparkling with excitement, and he danced around the room.

I was happy for him. He had been struggling with some depression. He never discussed why he was unhappy at times. I knew only that he was happiest when he was working. It brought him deep joy just to be talking about the Vanderbilt project.

"Come, come," he urged. "Let's get you up here on the pedestal and have you pose like an angel holding up something. No, that will not do," he said, more to himself. "Think of your arms reaching up to God."

As he worked the plaster, he was in deep concentration and humming a beautiful melody I had often heard him sing. His rich and velvety voice was calming. My mind wandered back to happy memories of my life in Stora Blåsjön. I recalled the many hours listening to Papa's stories about his adventures in the forests, the joys of living on our farm surrounded by beautiful trees, or celebrating the various holiday traditions with our relatives.

Suddenly, I was startled to hear Mr. Saint-Gaudens's voice. "Whatever you were doing or thinking, Albertina, your face was perfect. Do not stop. I just have a few things I want to improve on."

He stopped humming. Now I was only aware of how my neck and shoulders were throbbing. I tried to go back to the magical place I had been just a few minutes ago, but it was not meant to be.

"I am sorry, sir. I think I need to rest awhile."

He helped me step off the pedestal. I felt a surge of warmth flow through me when he took my hand.

"I become so absorbed in my work, I sometimes forget about everything else. I am sorry I was not aware of how tired you were becoming." He turned and looked at the clock. "My goodness! I did not know it had gotten so late. No wonder you are tired." He lightly kissed my hand. "Go home now and get some rest. Tomorrow is another day."

I returned to Hoboken with a lilt in my step, even though my body was aching and tired. I was excited for tomorrow to come.

The more I came to know Mr. Saint-Gaudens, the more I came to understand the intensity he brought to his art. I also came to understand that sometimes the intensity came with a price.

I learned that between 1879 and 1881, Mr. Saint-Gaudens, his brother, and some other workers were in Paris working on *Farragut Monument*. It was one of the most stressful times for all of them. It was Mr. Saint-Gaudens's first major commission, and it brought honor and recognition to one of America's naval heroes. Admiral Farragut was so respected and admired that President Grant attended his funeral. Therefore, Mr. Saint-Gaudens strove to create a monument that would give appropriate homage to this hero. The success of this monument brought Mr. Saint-Gaudens and Stanford White, his good friend and architect, well-deserved recognition.

Will Low, another good friend and an artist in his own right, was also there in Paris helping with this large monument. It was quite an ordeal to bring the magnificent statue to America. I learned that Mr. Saint-Gaudens had suffered severe pains in his stomach for several days. Evidently, it was the first of several episodes of inflammation in his intestines and stomach.

Despite the stress, *Farragut Monument* was a success. After the unveiling ceremony, as Mr. and Mrs. Saint-Gaudens was returning home, they saw an elderly man standing in front of the monument. It turned out to be Mr. Saint-Gaudens's father, Bernard.

It was Bernard who had first recognized his son's artistic talent. He arranged for an apprenticeship with a renowned cameo cutter, Louis Avet, when Augustus was thirteen. His parents also encouraged and helped their son to go to Paris to study art in 1867.

Mr. Saint-Gaudens later told me how touched he was to see his father standing there. He said, "It is a sight I shall never forget."

The sky was blue, the sounds of the birds were happy, and the sweet aroma of blooming trees and flowers filled the air. As I approached the door to the studio, I saw Mrs. Saint-Gaudens standing there. I do not know if she was waiting for me, but I suspect she was.

I approached her with a curtsy. "Good morning, madam."

She stood tall and straight, with a somber look on her face and her hands tightly folded at her waist. In a loud and stern manner, she said, "Miss Hultgren, I want you to understand that your posing for my husband's work is only a job. I advise you to not let your youth and beauty, nor any feelings of infatuation, interfere with your work."

I stood there frozen in time, not sure how to respond. I only nodded, kept my eyes cast down, and curtsied again. "Yes, madam."

"That is all. Now go on up and do your job. Not a word about this conversation to my husband. Do you understand?"

I whispered, "Yes, madam," still feeling quite confused.

I stood and watched Mrs. Saint-Gaudens walk away. Then I slowly stepped into the studio. Immediately I heard Mr. Saint-Gaudens's voice.

"Albertina, what is wrong? You look as though you have seen a ghost."

I felt cold and clammy. My heart was rapidly beating, and my stomach was churning. I was overwhelmed by Mrs. Saint-Gaudens's words and tone. What had I said or done for her to talk to me that way?

"Please, sir, may I be excused from working today? I do not feel at all well. I will come back tomorrow."

I could not even look at him. I knew he would see I was not being completely honest with him.

I turned to leave through the door I had just entered, but I felt his hand on my shoulder. He leaned toward me and whispered in my ear.

"I do not know what my wife said to you, but please do not let her influence you."

His hand on my shoulder was warm and comforting, his breath in my ear pulsated loving energy, and his words were gentle and calming.

After a few moments, I looked up into his kind face. I nodded and whispered, "I will stay."

"Come with me." Mr. Saint-Gaudens offered his arm. "Let us take a walk."

We went but a few short blocks before he stopped at a stately home, walked us up the steps, and put a key in the door.

"This home belongs to a dear friend who is traveling in Europe right now. Whenever he travels, he leaves the keys with me so I might use it to get away from work or family." He smiled. "He has a beautiful garden, where I find peace and quiet. It inspires and calms me."

He chuckled to himself and waved me into an alcove of marble floors with a staircase leading to the upper floor. He escorted me through the main parlor and another set of doors to a small and private garden. A stone wall covered with ivy was just high enough for privacy. English red roses were blooming, two large azalea bushes were filled with buds ready to burst open with a pink explosion, and a brick path guided us to a bench in front of a small fountain.

"Oh, my," I said. "This is so beautiful and peaceful."

"I do not share it with many people, because it is my place of solitude. Even my dear wife, Gussie, has not been here, nor does she know about it."

"Mr. Saint-Gaudens—" I started, but he interrupted me.

"Now you must call me Gus. I do not like such formality, especially from you."

For the next glorious hour we sat on the bench, walked the garden grounds, then sat some more as we discussed my posing, his work, and his wife's role, or lack thereof. He talked about his passion for his various works of art, from the smallest broach to the largest statue.

"I love to create," he simply said. "Art and working with my hands means everything to me. I believe I was born to do this."

He was so knowledgeable and had traveled to many of the surrounding states, as well as to Ireland, England, France, and Italy. He spoke fluent French and Gaelic, and a little Italian. He was raised in the home of a French father and Irish mother, and they both spoke their native tongues.

He told me that when he was about nineteen years old, he went to live in Paris studying at the École gratuite de Dessin and then later the École des Beaux-Arts. He traveled through parts of France and Italy and did not return to New York City until fall 1872, at the age of twenty-four.

"I had studied hard and felt ready to begin my career in earnest," he said. "I knew my calling was in the art of sculpture."

After a while, we sat in silence, taking in the smells of the air, the various colors surrounding us, and the sounds gently whispering in our ears.

"I do not want to end this very special time," he eventually said with a sadness in his voice but also a kind smile, "but I am afraid we must get to work."

CHAPTER 8

THE MISTRESS

1882

I was spending more days at the studio, so I followed Gus's suggestion to get a place in the city. I moved from the farm in Hoboken to a three-room apartment at 143 West Forty-Fifth Street. It was not far from the studio.

I made the move much to the protestations of my entire family.

"Mother, I am a woman now and quite capable of taking care of myself," I told her. "Living near the studio will make life so much easier. I will still come to visit you often."

Mother's frown of concern never changed. "How can you afford a place in the big city?"

"Mother, I have told you—I make twenty-five dollars per month modeling for Mr. Saint-Gaudens, plus I get a little more when I model for Louis or other artists. My rent is only ten dollars per month."

"Albertina, this is not right. You must think about your reputation!" Mother huffed in full Swedish now. "First you change your name, and now you leave your family. What is next, Albertina? What is next?"

She gave me no chance to reply. She stood up and glared at me.

"What would your dear papa say about all this? I have failed you as a mother." She turned on her heel and left the room.

For the next few days, she avoided me.

My new apartment was just blocks from the Sherwood Studio Building. I loved living independently, without the watchful eyes of both my mother and aunt. However, I did miss the closeness of the wooded areas around the farm.

I brought my bed and chest of drawers from the farm. I then bought a settee and table, essential wares for the kitchen, some cotton lace curtains, and a vase so I could brighten the room with flowers whenever possible. On the wall above my bed, I hung a picture of our farm in Sweden that my grandmother had painted so many years ago. I was very proud of my new place.

One Sunday, Mother came to visit me. It was a wonderful surprise. I was so proud and happy to show her my place. As we walked through the three rooms, she would mutter, "Very nice," or "Oh, yes," or "How pretty." When she saw Grandma's painting of Stora Blåsjön, she sighed.

"That is so far away, but the memories are so vivid. I am glad to see you have hung Grandma's painting."

She soon began to smile and relax as we sat for some tea. I asked about Ingrid and Nels.

"Your uncle is not doing well at all. I am most concerned about him, but he continues to refuse to see a doctor." She looked up at me and asked, "Could you come out to the farm sometime soon? You might be able to encourage him."

"Yes, of course." My heart sank for my dear Nels, who was like a father to me.

Over time, Mother came to accept my new life, but she cautioned me, "You are walking on a dangerous path that could lead to heartbreak and loneliness. This is not what Papa or I would choose for you, but please know that I love you with all my heart and I am always here for you."

Mother and I had never lived apart. I knew it was hard for her to accept my decision to move. My living apart from her meant she no longer had control over my choices or actions. I was sure this frightened her. There were so many changes in a short period of time.

I reached out to her with a long embrace. *"Jag älskar dig, Mor,"* I said, speaking in our native language with the deepest affection and love.

The tenants next door were Helen and Frank Tutschek, who had been married seven years. They were a kind couple, welcoming me into the building and making me feel most at home. I often spent time with Helen, who was busy with her six-year-old son whenever he was not in school. She was a lively and introspective lady. We went shopping together and had tea and biscuits in one of our apartments.

Early on she asked, "What do you do for a living, Albertina? You're often gone for many hours a day, but then other days you are home." She laughed at her own question. "I'm a nosey sort of person, aren't I? Well, Frank says I need to mind own business."

I laughed too. "No, you are not nosey. I am a model for a sculptor here in the city. Some days he needs me for longer hours than other days."

Over the years, she learned more about me and I about her. Our friendship started out easily and continued to only deepen.

Shortly after my move, Gus too surprised me with a visit. He walked in with one hand behind his back, gave me a kiss on the cheek, and nodded his head.

"Oh, very nice. You have brought beauty to this otherwise rather drab room." With a slight bow, he presented a bouquet of white daisies. "A little gift to bring in sunshine and chase away any shadows that might try to appear."

We sat on the settee. I found myself quite nervous, fidgeting with the hem of my apron. I knew it was quite improper for a gentleman to be alone with a woman in her residence.

Seeing my nervousness, Gus placed his hand on top of mine. "Albertina, please do not worry or be nervous. I know it is wrong for me to be here, but I could not stop thinking about you."

I nodded and looked at him with a slight smile. "Would you like some tea? I do not have any coffee."

We drank our tea and talked about the weather, about the Vanderbilt mantelpiece, and Uncle Nels's health. Soon we were both quiet. I was not sure what to say or do.

He rubbed his hands together and turned toward me. "I must be honest. I wanted to see you." He took both my hands in his and kissed them so gently. He whispered, "My angel."

With one hand, he lifted my chin so we could gaze into each other's eyes. He repeated, "My angel," then gently placed his lips onto mine.

I started to pull away, but I could not resist his embrace and kiss. I enjoyed the physical sensations of warmth flowing through every part of my body. I returned his kisses with all the love I had in my heart.

When Gus began to unbutton my dress, I thought I would faint from the heat traveling through me. I stepped back, and we looked into each other's eyes as he continued to undress me. Once he had removed my dress, he removed his jacket, shirt, and pants.

He then guided me into the bedroom, where he removed my bodice and began to explore my breasts with his lips and hands. I drifted into another universe of deep love, passion, and physical sensations I had never experienced.

Suddenly, he stopped and rose up on one elbow from my trembling body. "I do not want to hurt you in any way." He looked deeply into my eyes and asked, "Are you all right?"

I nodded, unable and unwilling to resist his touches and tender words. My heart was about to explode, and my body screamed for this moment to never end.

He continued to explore my body with tenderness and murmured words of love. Upon his inserting his private part, I first felt some pain, then quickly my body burst with sensations I had never felt before. It was as if my body traveled to a new dimension of heat, tingling, and pulsations. I had gone to heaven and slowly drifted back to earth as we embraced each other.

The rest of the afternoon, we held each other and kissed, and he taught me how to enjoy his body.

My beautiful memories of our lovemaking created some new, unexpected emotions. I suddenly struggled with jealousy that Gussie had a child with Gus, yet I was without a child, let alone a husband.

I knew Maria could help me sort out the feelings. "I should not be so hurt," I told her. "After all, she is his wife, and I have no legal or moral claim to him." I sighed. "Someday I would like to have Gus's child, but I know that unless we were married that cannot be."

I gazed out the window and thought about how different our lives would be if such a situation should ever occur.

Maria pulled me out of my reverie as if she knew what I was thinking. "My sweet child, be careful what you wish for. We live in an age where children born out of wedlock are not welcome into society. They are called bastards, and other children can be quite mean to them. And while society will turn its head when a man has a mistress, it will not look upon him with any kindness if he leaves his wife and has a child. It could be very costly to Gus's career, which I am sure you know is his great love and passion."

I knew she was right. I did not want to do anything to jeopardize his career or reputation.

CHAPTER 9

NEW BEGINNINGS

1883–84

The Brooklyn Bridge opened in 1883 with great fanfare. It was an accomplishment not to be duplicated for many years. It provided easy access to New York City for cars, buggies, and people.

That same year, the Metropolitan Opera House opened. Gus had been very supportive of the project. We managed to attend a couple of performances by going there separately but sitting in the same box. Gus bought me a pair of beautiful pearl-handled opera glasses that folded down into a leather case. I was speechless with joy and gratitude. I kissed him on each cheek, his forehead, the tip of his nose, and then down to his narrow lips, where I lingered a little longer.

In awe, I watched the performance of Mozart's *The Magic Flute*, one of Gus's favorite operas. He introduced me to his close friend Stanford White, who designed several pedestals on which Gus's sculptures stood. I liked Mr. White immediately, and he insisted I call him Stanford. I could tell right away that he was quite the ladies' man—always giving a wink, a flirtatious smile, or a kiss to many of the women. He was exuberant, full of energy, and humorous. He was a joy to be around.

That same year, Stanford and Gus traveled to New Mexico for a vacation and a time to gather inspiration. Gus wrote about his adventures in the town of Engle, where a store caught fire next to their lodging. It was a dangerous experience, with gun cartridges exploding and the loss of everything in the store. The next morning, they took a stagecoach through the desert and mountains to join Stanford's brother, Dick, who was a miner. He led them on horseback to his mine and cabin some twenty-five miles farther from town.

It was a rough trip but well worth it. During the few days they stayed with Dick, they ate deer jerky and delicious soups, and they camped while hunting for deer. They explored the mine and met the four other miners, who were rough, hardworking, and loud. Gus sent me postcards every day with words of his love. The photos showed white sands with a starkness that created a beauty all its own.

They also traveled to Santa Fe on the Atchison, Topeka, and Santa Fe Railway, in one of the new trains designed and developed to meet the needs of the genteel class. They stopped and ate at one of the many Harvey House restaurants. There the Harvey Girls, who brought the concept of respectability to restaurants in the Old West, served them delicious food. He sent a photograph of him and Stanford standing on each side of a pretty blond waitress.

I must admit, I wished I had been the woman standing in the middle of such handsome, talented, and friendly (perhaps too much at times) gentlemen. That was the extent of my jealousy, though. I did not care that Gus might be with other women on this trip—or at any other time. I knew Gus had had many affairs in the past. One had been quite serious with a woman named Angelina. He had met her before meeting and marrying Mrs. Saint-Gaudens. If Gus now had interludes with other women, then they were brief. I accepted them as outlets for his sexual desires only. I knew our relationship was deep and true, and that is where I kept my heart and mind.

Gus and Stanford stayed in Santa Fe for a few days. They visited with the artists and writers there, who felt the town—with its natural beauty, solitude, and dry climate—was the perfect place to develop their talents. I smiled and laughed at some of the cartoons Gus drew of the local people, the Indians, and Stanford.

I was lonely for Gus. I tried to keep busy just walking around New York City. I often walked by the studio at 148 West Thirty-Sixth Street, hoping to run into one of Gus's workers. I missed the excitement, creativity, and sights and smells of the studio. I especially missed Louis.

One day, I saw Louis coming out the front door just as I was approaching. His head was down and his eyes were downcast.

"Good afternoon, Louis." I smiled and held out my hand.

It took a short time for him to recognize me. He appeared to be coming out of a dreamlike state.

"Oh, my dear Albertina—it is so good to see you." He slightly smiled and asked, "Are you here to do some work?"

I started to reply, but he quickly continued in a bit of a monotone voice.

"We have been working quite hard on the beginnings of two projects. Gus is traveling frequently, meeting with a variety of businessmen, politicians, and who knows who else."

Louis kept turning his hat around while holding it by its brim. His hair looked uncombed, his clothing was quite wrinkled, and he had a slight beard growing. He often kept his eyes cast down and seemed to have difficulty looking me in the eye.

"It is so good to see you, Louis. I have missed you," I said while putting my hand on one of his. "Perhaps you can come to my place with Gus some time. I will fix a delicious Swedish dessert to go with our tea. Would you like that?"

He nodded and began to shift from side to side. "Perhaps I will, but now I must be on my way." He suddenly turned and walked away.

I was surprised and concerned about his mannerisms and unkempt look. I watched him walk away, then turned around and strolled back in the direction of home.

Fortunately, I had my parasol open above my head, because I suddenly heard Gussie's loud and gruff voice, saying, "Where did he go? He cannot just walk away from his work."

I lowered my parasol to cover my face and quickly walked into a dress shop. I do not believe Gussie saw me, or else I am sure I would have heard her wrath.

When Gus returned from New Mexico a few days later, I told him about the whole incident.

"Do not worry, my dear," he said. "I am quite convinced Gussie did not see you. Yet perhaps it would be best if you not go to the studio for a while. Despite all her treatments and cures, she just does not feel well. She has not been easy to live with."

He sat quietly for a few minutes, then shook his head. "I know my brother is having great difficulty now with his feelings about himself—his fears and insecurities. He does not believe he is the talented, kind, and beautiful person he is. I am concerned about him and am looking into some kind of help for him."

We sat in silence for a few minutes.

"I have tried to talk about my concerns for him with our father," Gus continued, "but Father does not seem to want to listen. He never responds. He just quickly changes the subject. I am sure it brings back too many sad memories of my dear mama, so the burden is on me."

Gus shared that both he and his brother had always struggled with bouts of depression and how their mother too often had times of great melancholy.

"I guess Louis and I are more like our mother than our father. I have so much to be grateful for, yet there are days or weeks when I cannot rise above the depression."

Gus got up and went to the window, silently watching people going about their business.

"Years ago, I gave Louis a lot of responsibility to get *Hiawatha* shipped out of Rome, which meant handling the arrangements and finances. But he just could not do it. He was overwhelmed."

He turned to me with tears in his eyes. He wiped them.

"Did you know that Louis disappeared for about two years? I think it began in 1876. We were all so worried about him, then he suddenly showed up. He told me he had been married, but his wife died while giving birth to their first child. Unfortunately, the baby also died. He was penniless and appeared to have a drinking problem with too much wine."

He remained quiet, then reminisced about how when they were boys, he used to protect Louis from bullies.

"He was always slender and shy, and he liked to be with me rather than make new friends. I encouraged him with his art, helping him to get into the École des Beaux-Arts in Paris. I taught him how to cut cameos and hired him to help me in the studios. You know he is very talented, but I am not sure he believes that. I have always been there for him, but sometimes he will not let me or anyone else help him. And now, what am I to do?"

"Gus, you have always been such a good and caring brother. Louis loves you more than words could ever begin to describe. I know he went to a sanitarium several years ago. Do you think it helped him? Is this something you are thinking of doing again?"

Suddenly, Gus came back to the sofa and sat down with a long sigh. He took my hand and kissed it.

"You are asking difficult questions. Yes, he did leave the sanitarium a more contented man and got back to work rather quickly." He paused and thought deeply. "But would a stay in the sanitarium be good for him now? I do not know. All of us have been working long hours with little rest, and it seems one problem after another keeps coming up. Louis cannot handle the stress as well as others can. Perhaps I will just send him to Toulouse, where our brother Andrew lives in France. Louis can relax there and work when he wants."

For a long time, we just sat quietly again.

"I am telling you, Gus—you are a kind and good man. Whatever you decide will be out of love for your brother."

"Do you know how much I love you and all that you mean to me? You are my angel and my inspiration. Do not ever forget that, and know that I will never leave you." He turned away a little and said in almost a whisper, "No matter how depressed I might get, promise me you won't let them put me in an institution."

I knew I would never be a part of such a decision. But I still said, "Yes, my love, I promise."

Chapter 10

New Identity

1883–84

It was a warm summer morning. I had spent a few days at the farm in Hoboken. I had taken an extra-long walk through the woods, enjoying the strong pine smells. Then I rode the ferry back into the city and let the gentle wind blow my hair freely away from my face. The water was blue-gray, and the short ride was mesmerizing. I tried to see if any water creatures would appear, though I prayed that no draugs, lindworms, or nøkkens would appear—any of which can be quite evil.

I walked into the studio with a smile. Each hour of posing was now easier. Whenever I needed to center myself, I could just relive my times in the woods or imagine the lovely garden where I spent the afternoon with Gus. I could forget all about the aches in my body, the hunger pangs in my stomach, or the occasional lightheadedness.

I was posing for a new project. Former New York governor Edwin Morgan had commissioned Gus to sculpt his tomb. The piece was to have three angels standing in front of a Greek cross. They each wore flowing gowns and garlands of flowers around their waists. The central angel also wore a wreath of flowers on her head. One held a scroll, another a lyre, and the third a harp.

Sometimes my hair was tightly bound in a bun sitting high on my head, while other times Gus took the pins out and ran his hands through my curly locks until it looked as though I had just been in a windstorm. In the end, he preferred my hair falling softly around my face. He would drape my body in loose-fitting gowns or put garlands and wreaths on my head.

"My dear Albertina," he said, "you have the gift to express so many emotions with your eyes or a slight change in your body posture. You can look like a stealthy cat on the hunt or a wild cat defending her cubs. Other times, you have a gaze of someone in rapture or someone seeing the eyes of God. Come over here," he said, gesturing. "I want to show you the initial plaster casts of the three angels for the sculpture for which you have been posing these past weeks."

Gus led me to where the three statues were standing. It was my first time to see them because Gus did not want me to be influenced by what he sculpted. I was astonished to see my face looking back at me from three different angels.

"When I was last in France, I selected the marble for them," he said with excitement.

Gus was very proud of his three angels. At long last, the completed marble angels were transferred to the Cedar Hill Cemetery just days before the tomb's scheduled unveiling in August 1884. But then the unspeakable happened: a fire broke out at the cemetery. The angels were destroyed. It was a heart-wrenching loss.

Thankfully, Gus still had plaster duplicates of two of the angels. He had begun to recreate the third angel and cast the others in marble when he received a message from Mr. Morgan's widow. Mr. Morgan had died in February 1883. From his deathbed, he had been very disappointed that his tomb had not been completed. And now Mrs. Morgan had changed her mind as to the design of the tomb. She wanted only one angel rather than all three.

Gus was enraged and hurt, but he quickly turned his focus to a new commission he hoped to win. It was to be *Standing Lincoln*, a piece in honor of Abraham Lincoln.

A week after the fire, Gus greeted me at the studio with a big smile and a lilt in his voice. "Right now I am working on some small reliefs and medallions besides making plans to secure the Lincoln statue commission. I have also received a commission for a Shaw memorial, which will keep me busy for some time. And I have my continuing work on *The Puritan*. But I have a recurring vision of an angel for which I want you to pose sometime in the near future. I will tell you more about this vision at a later time."

We stood there in silence for a while. He was looking at me to the point that I felt somewhat embarrassed. I was curious as to what he was thinking. His lips were slightly parted and his smile was warm and comforting. I began to relax and looked him in the eyes with all my deepest feelings spilling out.

"Do you have any idea how beautiful and angelic your face is? Of course you do not. No one sees themselves as others do." He looked at me intently as he talked. "My meeting you was a true gift from God."

He turned to face me. Our heads were so close I could feel his breath on my face. My whole body unexpectedly felt hot and began to shake. My knees weakened.

"Sir, you are most kind," I finally said.

"My dear child, there is nothing about you or what I said that should embarrass you. Come here—let's sit for a minute and have some tea."

We sat at a small table with two wooden chairs. Gus poured the tea and asked, "Would you like to talk about why you got embarrassed when I said you were beautiful?"

I kept the teacup near my lips and murmured, "No, Mr. Saint-Gaudens."

He lightly laughed. "So, I am Mr. Saint-Gaudens again. What happened to calling me Gus?"

He watched me closely and saw a half smile go across my face behind the teacup.

"Albertina, you are beautiful. You have the perfect face and body for the type of sculpture I am doing. And there is nothing wrong with that." He reached across the table, took the teacup out of my hands, and sweetly said, "There is but one thing I would like to change about you."

I looked up. "What? I mean, what would you change?"

"Your name, my sweet thing. Your name, Albertina Hultgren, is a mouthful." He lightly laughed again. "I do not mean to offend you, but it sounds like a name for an old woman from Sweden."

We both laughed at this, though I was not exactly sure what he meant by this question about names.

"I have been thinking about this for some time." he continued. "It is equally important that my model have a name as beautiful as she. I hope you can understand what I am trying to say."

He paused and searched my face for some reaction. I could only listen and try to grasp what the meaning of all this was.

"Would you like to know what name I have chosen for you?"

I was quite startled and quickly looked up at him with my mouth agape. Gus sat back in his chair, giving me time to finally nod and whisper a yes. I adored him and trusted him, so I would of course want to hear this name he had created for me.

He stood up, swept one arm toward me, and bowed. To an imaginary group of people, he announced, "May I introduce the fair lady, Davida."

His eyes sparkled, and he excitedly waited for my response. I just stared for a long moment. In my silence, he went on to explain.

"*David* is a statue by Michelangelo. It is the most handsome and perfectly sculpted piece of art I have ever seen. David's body is naked and perfect, standing in Florence, and everyone marvels at this great sculpture." Gus knelt down and put his strong hands over my folded hands in my lap. "You are the female answer to David. You are as beautiful in the face and perfect in the body as David was handsome and perfect."

He suddenly stood up and began to pace the room. He muttered names to himself and often stopped and stroked his beard.

"Now we need to think about a last name instead of Hultgren. Perhaps you have some ideas?"

My head was spinning, and I could not think of what to say. I was so confused. "I only know Swedish names or those of people I have met here in America," I finally said.

"Are there names you like?"

"Well, I guess I like all the names."

Gus laughed. "A better question might be, what is the last name of someone you truly like or admire? Tell me some names, and I will see if they go with Davida."

I relaxed a little as I thought about the people I liked. "Well, I consider Ms. Maria Johnson a wonderful friend I completely trust and admire. My aunt Ingrid is another person, but her last name is Petersson."

I paused and smiled before saying, "I do respect and admire *you*, but I guess it would not be right to take your name."

We both laughed, and I felt a little embarrassed.

Each time I said a person's name, Gus would test the name with Davida. I kept searching my brain, recalling people I had met.

"There was a very nice woman who came aboard the ship when we docked in South Hampton," I remembered. "Her name was Mrs. Arleigh Clark, a recent widow going to Canada to live with her daughter. She and Mother became fast friends, seeing as they were both widowed. She was most kind. I often think about her and wonder how she is, but I guess I will never know."

I paused and suddenly realized that Mrs. Clark and Maria were very much alike. They were both independent, friendly, intelligent, and very easy to talk to. I had known Mrs. Clark for only a short time, but she left a deep impression on me, just as Maria had.

Gus stroked his beard again. I could see his lips moving without any audible words coming out. Then he said, "Davida Clark Johnson." He repeated it a couple of times, then nodded and said, "Davida Johnson Clark. So now, what do you think about having that as your new name?"

His alluring eyes searched mine for some kind of response. I searched for words.

"I like it, but I do not think my mother will permit me to change my name. In our culture, names are very important. I was named for my grandfather, Albert Hallgren, who was a very fine man."

I began to tremble, thinking of Mother's likely reaction. My emotions went from excitement and happiness to fear and sadness.

Gus understood. "I do not want to upset you or hurt you. I am sorry."

He stood up and began to roll down his shirt sleeves as a symbolic sign that the day's conversation and work were over for him.

"Gus, may I have a few days to think about this? I will need to talk to Mother. You understand, don't you?" I was as concerned about hurting him as he was of me.

He nodded, smiled, and lightly kissed me on the cheek.

"Louis will work with you the rest of the day," he said. "I am already late for a meeting with Stanford."

As he walked out the door, bright sunshine spilled in, then darkness filled that side of the room, as well as my heart.

The rest of the afternoon was miserable because I could not concentrate. I could not seem to hold still, and too often my body would begin to shake.

Finally at one point, Louis said with frustration, "You can go home for the day, Albertina. I think we are both tired and need a rest. But do be here bright and early in the morning."

Once I was back in Hoboken, I quickened my pace to the woods near the farm. I was very relieved to escape into the forest. I knelt among the pine needles and leaned against my favorite large boulder. I removed my bonnet and shook my thick hair free.

My face was still flushed as I leaned my head back to let the filtered sunrays spread their healing energy across my furrowed brow. Behind my closed eyelids, I saw only red and some flashes of white light. All of this relaxed me enough so my heart and mind could listen to one another.

How much would changing my name upset Mother or the rest of

my family? Would my grandfather in heaven be angry or hurt? What about pleasing Gus? And what would make *me* happy? The answer to that last question was easy: I would do anything to make Gus happy.

I opened my eyes and suddenly saw beautiful flowers all around me. "These were not here before," I told myself. "Flowers do not grow in such a thick forest, where there is so little sunlight."

When I reached out to touch the blue flower nearest me, it suddenly became a fairy. She had long flowing hair with a floral wreath sitting on top of her head. She was quite beautiful and radiating light. I knew that sometimes fairies or skogsrån can be dangerous, but I saw love radiating from this particular fairy.

"How can this be? Am I dreaming?" I asked.

"No, you are not dreaming. It is your heart talking to you," the fairy replied. "Sometimes the only way the heart can be heard over the rational mind is to replace the rational with the imaginary."

I sat up straight and rubbed my eyes. I was sure that when I opened them, the fairy and flowers would all be gone. But that was not the case when I opened my eyes.

"You are still here," I said.

"Follow your heart. As long as you follow your heart with unconditional love, then it is never wrong." This magical creature watched me closely before she continued. "Do not let other people—with their moral platitudes, man-made laws, and shortsightedness keep you from doing what is right for you."

She paused a long time, allowing me to think.

"Davida, follow your heart."

I looked up, startled upon hearing my new name. Suddenly the pine trees stood mightily with the sunrays peeking through their outstretched boughs. There were no flowers, only pine needles and pinecones. I left the forest with a smile and repeatedly whispered the name Davida.

I went to Maria's home and told her about my new name. She was so touched to hear I had taken her name as my own. And when I told her everything Gus had shared with me that day, she gently laughed.

"My dear Albertina—I mean, Davida—remember that you are your own woman and making your own decisions. Hold your head up high and believe in yourself and the journey in which you are embarking."

"Oh, Maria, what would I do without you? You understand me, and you never judge me." I sighed and sat quietly thinking about what she had just said.

"Tell me about Mr. Saint-Gaudens," she said with a wise smile. "Even though I know him socially, is there anything about him that you want to share?"

I was surprised at first by her question. But as I talked about Gus, I understood the purpose. As only a dear friend could do, she helped me see why I respected, admired, and cared for Gus.

"Well, he is most charming and very friendly to everyone. I do not think there is anyone who does not like him." A few moments went by before I continued. "He has a certain wit about him. He likes to tell jokes and be playful with others. Every day, he draws cartoons, which he mainly gives to his wife."

Mentioning his wife brought a feeling of concern or disturbance, which I did not fully understand at the time.

I shook my head to be rid of the memories of our last meeting when she threatened me. After a short pause I continued, "From what I hear and see, it appears that Gus is very good to Mrs. Saint-Gaudens and that he does have a certain kind of love and respect for her."

I decided to speak of more positive things. Even though Maria knew Gus fairly well, I wanted to impress upon her that he was a kind and loving husband, brother, and friend.

"Now, Gus certainly loves and respects his brother Louis, who is always very nice to me. He is a most kind and gentle man, but I think he has a bit of a drinking problem, perhaps because of some depression. Some mornings he looks as though he has not slept at all, with his clothes quite rumpled and not clean. I have heard the workers say things. And once I overheard Gus say to Louis, 'If you are going to work here for me, you are not going to drink heavily the night before.' I know Gus truly cares about his brother and is sometimes tough on him as a way of trying to help."

Between the chamomile tea, the conversation, and Maria's loving presence, I was relaxed and eager to talk more, especially about Gus. "Did you know Gus loves to sing? In fact, he has a beautiful voice that is deep and rich. He always sings while he works. I think it is one of the things I love about him. I know that if he is singing, then he is happy, and that makes my heart rejoice."

I leaned back in the chair and looked out the window, smiling as I thought about him.

"Where are you now in your thoughts?" Maria asked, smiling herself. "Wherever you are, I can see happiness in your eyes."

"Oh, Maria, I know I am young and Gus is quite a bit older and wiser than me. I am a girl from a small village in Sweden, and he is a famous and well-respected artist. But I think I love him." I started to cry and laugh at the same time. "I love him, because he is kind, gentle, and sweet. He is talented, intelligent, and humble. I watch him while he sketches, chisels, or instructs his workers. I love him the most when he suddenly stops singing and stares off in the distance—I know his mind is creating a beautiful work of art. During those moments, no one disturbs him. It is as if he is listening to God."

"I am sure God is talking to him at those moments. Great art is the work of God's hands working through an artist's hands, such as those of Mr. Saint-Gaudens."

I listened to the clock ticking on the mantle. Time was going by, time that would never be retrieved.

"I trust Gus and I love him. I do not think he loves me, but that does not matter. Whatever happens, I now know my love for him will see me through anything."

CHAPTER 11

CHALLENGES

1884–85

Gus began to work on *The Puritan* with renewed vigor. It would later be recognized as one of his greatest accomplishments. Chester Chapin, a railroad tycoon and congressman, commissioned Gus to do a statue of his ancestor Deacon Samuel Chapin, an early settler in Springfield, Massachusetts. Gus did a lot of research and chose one of Chester Chapin's relatives to inspire the statue's face. He hired a tall, muscular, and symmetrical young man to pose for the statue's body. He used paintings and carvings of typical Puritan attire to get the correct look.

Work had first begun in the Sherwood Studio Building on Fifth-Seventh Street, but it later moved to the Thirty-Sixth Street studio, where Gus had also begun preliminary work to secure the Lincoln statue commission. He worked such long hours and at such high speed that he often fell asleep at the studio or at my apartment immediately after a light supper. He would be stretched across the settee, with his head resting on one end and his stocking feet dangling from the other. I would watch him sleep and listen to his deep breaths and occasional snorts. I treasured these times when he was all mine.

Other evenings, I would listen to both his complaints and his praises about his workers, the studio space, or the clients or committees who gave him the various commissions. He was a perfectionist and did not tolerate anything less from anyone.

He was also grateful for Gussie's help with keeping the finances straight despite her health issues. And despite all his commissions, he was well aware that they still occasionally found themselves in a precarious financial situation. Gus was not always paid a start-up fund; rather, he would be paid in full once the commission was completed. However, he had workers, rent, and material costs to pay up front. Marble was often his highest expense.

Gussie was perhaps getting suspicious about Gus and me, even though they had not lived together for some time. Gus set up a small room in the Sherwood studio, where he lived most of the time when he was not with me.

These were times of such happiness for both of us. Occasionally we took walks. To those who saw us, we were just an ordinary couple in love. If they recognized Gus, we did not care.

The times Gus was traveling, I would make my way to Hoboken and spend several days with Aunt Ingrid, Uncle Nels, and Mother. It was a wonderful time, especially when I was helping in the garden or the kitchen. We would make raggmunk, meatballs, sweet-and-sour cabbage, and Swedish almond tarts. Our meals were happy times sharing laughter, stories, and remembrances of our lives in Sweden.

Every chance I got, I went to the nearby woods. There the same fairy often visited me. Each time, I fell into a dreamlike state.

She knew everything about my life. One day, she said, "A couple of big changes are coming that might affect your life. If you remain true in your love, and if you are patient, the events will only be life lessons from which you can learn."

It was my twenty-third birthday that December. At the last minute, Gus had to cancel his plans to spend the day with me. I decided to treat myself to an early supper at Delmonico's. I invited my neighbor Helen Tutschek, whose husband was away on business.

What a delightful time we had. We shared a bottle of red wine to go with our delicious Italian food. Helen was born and raised in New York City and marveled at all the changes that had taken place in her lifetime.

"The streets are so busy, and there are so many new and large buildings," she exclaimed. Her shoulders suddenly shuttered. "And oh, I still have nightmares about the earthquake this summer. It was so frightening. Thankfully we were all safe."

I nodded. "I have never been in anything like that before."

"Let's change the subject. This is too dreary." Helen looked around the room, took a sip of wine, then instructed, "Tell me about your work as a model. It all sounds so fascinating."

"It is hard work just trying to hold one position for a long period of time," I explained.

"Surely it can't be that hard," she said. "I should think it would be nice to just sit quiet for a while."

I laughed. "Well, it is not like sitting in a comfy chair reading a book. Here—I will prove it to you." I quickly looked around the room and saw that it was not very full of people. "Now sit straight," I directed her. "Hold your glass of wine as if you are about to drink it, but do not move until I tell you to."

She did as I said. I smiled as I watched her expression change as the time wore on.

After only a few minutes, she exclaimed, "My arm is tired, and my back is aching! Please may I move?"

We both began to laugh, and we each took a generous swallow of our wine.

"I will never again question how tiring your profession is," she said.

Over the years, Helen and I would have many enjoyable times together. She loved to laugh and did not take the world too seriously.

Gus was acquainted with Helen and her husband, seeing as they lived so near the studio. He was so pleased that I had such good friends in the big city. Helen and I had many talks about my relationship with Gus, to which she often said, "He is lucky to have your love just as you are. Such deep love only comes along once in a lifetime."

Gus and I often just sat and talked about our upbringings, parents, and families. Our lives started out worlds apart. Gus was born in Dublin, Ireland, to his Irish mother and French father.

"You remind me of my dear mother," he said. "She had a long, beautiful face and graceful hands with the most delicate fingers." Gus gazed out the window, and his eyes grew misty. "You remind me of her with your fair skin and the same kind of beauty."

I laid my head upon his shoulder and squeezed his hand. "You loved her very much, and I am sure you miss her."

Gus took out his handkerchief, wiped his eyes, then gently blew his nose. "She had such a lilt to her voice with her Irish accent. To my ears, it was like listening to an angel sing."

Suddenly, he laughed and continued, "Of course, when she was angry and had to discipline any of us boys, her voice no longer sounded like an angel's. One day, when I was about eleven or twelve years old, she thought I was being a little too sassy. I probably was, though at the time I did not think so. She grabbed the paddle out of the kitchen cupboard and raised her arm up to smack me on the rear."

Gus smiled as his memories flooded his mind.

"Now mind you, my mother was a small, little lady standing only about five foot. I was then just a tad taller. With a smile and glint in my eye, I gently wrapped one hand around her right wrist and took the paddle away from her with one swift move. 'Mother, I do not think we need this paddle anymore.'"

By now, Gus was laughing. "Mother looked up at me, then she broke into laughter and said, 'Son, I think you are right. But no more sass is to come out of that mouth again!' We hugged and began to dance around the kitchen."

Suddenly, I found myself doing some form of an Irish jig with Gus as we danced and laughed around the living room. Soon we were out of breath and collapsed onto the settee.

"Now tell me about your father," I insisted once we had caught out breaths.

"I so wish you could meet him, but I am afraid Father would never approve of our relationship. He often comes to the studio. I think he still misses Mother, though she died about ten years ago. He spends most of his time continuing to work at his shoemaking business or going to the local tavern, where he often drinks too much." Gus shook his head, ran his hand through his hair, and smiled. "Father can be such a tough person, hard to talk to. Yet when I think of how he has found the American dream, coming all the way from the little village of Aspet in the French Pyrenees, I am in awe of all he has accomplished."

I interrupted Gus, "Your father was born in France, right?" Gus nodded, so I then asked, "If your mother was in Ireland and your father was in France, how did they meet?"

"Now that is an interesting story in itself. Father had spent a few years in London after learning his shoemaking skills in Paris. He wanted to eventually have his own shop, so he made his way around Europe as a journeyman, eventually spending time in Dublin. There my mother made a living making buttonholes for shoes. Her work was exquisite, and her beautiful face and demeanor attracted him. So, one thing led to another, and they married just three months after meeting." Gus stopped, then pointed at himself. "And here I am."

"What a beautiful love story. I wish I could have met your mother. And I pray that someday I can tell your father how much I love his son.

In 1885, Gus was busy with three projects at different stages. He worked on getting the contract for the Lincoln statue in Chicago, he started *Shaw Memorial*, and he put the finishing touches on *The Puritan*.

Standing Lincoln required Gus to make a few trips to Chicago, and I went with him. We rode the train. It was very exciting to see the upper plains from New York to Illinois. The landscape of large farms and expansive fields with various crops was so different from anything I had seen before.

Gus had great admiration for President Lincoln. He remembered the day when as a young man he watched the procession with Lincoln's body go by. It was an image he would never forget. "It is important to capture the strength, gentleness, and leadership of this great man," Gus said as he worked on sketches and plans.

One day, we strolled along Fifty-Third Street in Hyde Park in the heart of Chicago, stopping in stores and pressing our noses against the shop windows. At one point, Gus took my hand and guided me into a jewelry store, where the glass cases were filled with earrings, necklaces, and rings that sparkled with a variety of jewels. I gasped at the beauty of it all.

Gus surprised me when he said to the clerk, "I want to buy your most beautiful ring for my wife." He put his arm around my waist and pulled me close to him. He looked longingly into my eyes and whispered, "In my heart, you are my wife."

Despite my whispered protests, Gus picked out a ring with two diamonds on each side of a blue sapphire. He slipped it onto my right ring finger, then kissed me so gently on my lips that I almost swooned.

CHAPTER 12

Lincoln, Shaw, Adams

1885

The year also brought some big changes, many of which caused me stress, worry, and loneliness. In the early spring, Gus, Gussie, and Homer moved to Cornish, New Hampshire. Each year during the warmer seasons, they rented a house, some buildings, and land there.

He still visited me as often as possible, but our love was tested when he told me Gussie had recently had a miscarriage that summer. I was jealous that Gussie still had a sexual relationship with him and had gotten pregnant. I so wanted a child but knew that such a pregnancy would cause both Gus and me untold stress and problems.

Gussie's miscarriage increased her depression and therefore increased her demands on Gus. He was constantly exhausted, he had trouble sleeping, and he became irritable over what appeared to be minor things.

"I do not know what to do," he told me during one visit to New York. "I must find a solution to this, so I can get back to my work and be there for both you and my family."

He held his head in his hands. I could see them slightly tremble. I reached over, gently touched his hands, and leaned my head onto his shoulder.

"My dear," he said, "I am torn between my love for you and my desire not to hurt Gussie. At times when I am with Gussie, I feel such guilt that I swear to myself I will never see you again and be a true and honest husband. But then, after a short time away from you, I know I cannot let you out of my life."

My heart was breaking for the man I loved so much. I had always known this situation would come. I had dreaded it. I had talked many times to Maria and Mother about my forbidden love with Gus. Now the day had come.

"Gus, let me ask you a question—but you must hear it as my pledge of love and devotion to you."

He looked at me with fear in his eyes.

"Just hear me out, please."

I waited until he seemed to relax his body a little.

"With love, there is always sacrifice. That is something my parents taught me. My father sacrificed his parents' love and approval when he married Mother without their blessing. And now, this torment you are going through because of our love—it is torment for me. According to society and the church, our love is wrong."

"It is not wrong—" he began.

"No, let me finish," I countered back. I took a deep breath. "I will move away. I will be out of your life, so you can rebuild your marriage before Gussie finds out about me. She may even now be suspicious. I do not know. But I do know her health would improve if she were at peace and could see and feel your complete love for her." I fought back the tears and struggled to get my words out. "I could start a new life away from New York. My selfish desire to be the only woman in your life is not love. For your peace, for Gussie's health, and for your career, I will make this sacrifice."

Gus sat on the settee and buried his face in his hands, crying as I had never heard anyone before.

After a few minutes, I said, "You know this is for the best." I kept repeating it.

Then we sat quietly side by side for a long time. All I could hear was our breathing, the building creaking, the radiator hissing off and on, and the street below bustling. When the clock chimed six times, I looked up in surprise that so much time had passed.

Gus rose, got his hat and coat, and stepped to the door. He paused with his hand on the doorknob. He softly spoke.

"I must think about what you have said. Please promise me you will not do anything until I have time to make a decision." He began to choke on his words. "I love you very much, my angel."

For a long week, I did not hear from Gus. I was miserable, not knowing how he was and not being able to reach out to him. I had long talks with Helen, who encouraged me to be strong and to believe that Gus would make the right decision for all concerned.

"Be patient, my dear. Sometimes the right decisions are the hardest ones." Helen put her arms around me and let me cry on her shoulder.

Because Chicago had such special memories for me, I made tentative plans to move to Chicago, a large city where I could find employment and afford a place to live.

Then one day, Gus appeared at my door. I had mixed emotions of joy and fear. By his face, I was not sure what would be the outcome of his visit. Was this a final farewell or a return with a new life ahead of us?

"I have left Cornish and moved back into the apartment on Thirty-Sixth Street."

I drew in a breath. Now I was free to come to his apartment or he to mine.

"I am more selfish and not as strong as you," he said. "I cannot let you go, but I also cannot end my marriage. I need to think about Homer as well as Gussie. Please do not leave me."

Shaw Memorial was a special project in Boston to commemorate Robert Gould Shaw and his all-black regiment, the Fifty-Fourth Massachusetts Volunteer Infantry that fought during the Civil War. To get the commission, Gus had to appear a happily married man, so he spent more time at home with Homer and Gussie in Cornish or New York. This was critically important to his image for the puritanical

Bostonians.

He was very grateful and excited about this opportunity, though, because it would pay handsomely and it sparked his creativity as never before. He set up a studio at 148 West Thirty-Sixth Street for this one memorial. Gus fixed the studio into two rooms, painted the walls, and added a skylight. This project would take some fourteen years to complete.

Gus shared his ideas of how the design for the memorial would look. He took a folded piece of paper from his coat pocket to show me his sketch.

"I envision Shaw riding his horse, leading his soldiers. An angel is flowing above them, as if guiding them. Shaw must look strong and confident; his soldiers equally brave and proud. And the angel will radiate love and protection." He stopped suddenly and looked at me. "What do you think? Do you see what I am seeing?"

I nodded enthusiastically and smiled, loving every moment. His passion for this project was more than any I had seen before.

"I want to recruit different black men to pose as the soldiers. The beautiful features of the Negro men can only be captured with them as the models. Therefore, I will have to spend a lot of days in Boston. I want the Negro men to be from Massachusetts, just as Shaw's men."

We talked about slavery and the injustice of it. Coming from Sweden, I had no experience with slavery. I heard about it only after I came to America. Gus had never lived or even visited the Southern part of the United States, so he too did not understand how some people could think they had the right to enslave other people.

"I have lived here in New York pretty much my whole life, and in my travels to Europe, I was never exposed to the concept of slavery. What gives one man the right to other men and make them work for him?"

We had no answers, but we both agreed that *Shaw Memorial* was an opportunity to give the Negro his proper place in history during the Civil War.

I traveled once to Boston. Gus and I registered at Young's Hotel on different days and had our own rooms. The hotel was quite beautiful with an interesting history of originally being the site of the Cornhill Coffee-House. With electric lights installed in 1881, it had one of the most beautiful and longest dining rooms.

I could enjoy the dining room during the afternoon meals, when Gus was busy working. I sat and watched the gentry, wondering what their stories might be. Was that a married couple? What kind of business did that certain gentleman have? Where were they from? What were their secrets?

In the privacy of my room in the evening, Gus was filled with genuine excitement and enthusiasm as he talked about recruiting men to pose.

"Now imagine this: here is a white man approaching a Negro to do some work for him right off the street." He laughed a little as he recalled, "Their eyes would shift side to side. They would take a few steps back, then turn away quickly, saying, 'No thanks, sir.' This was happening time and time again, until finally one man agreed to do it. I told that man how the others appeared afraid of me and would not even listen to me. That man said, 'Well, sir, slavery was legally abolished in 1864, but most of us are still treated as slaves and are fearful of the white man.'"

"So, why did that man accept your invitation to work for you?" I asked.

"The man told me, 'I thought you looked pretty trusting, and I got very interested when you said it was for General Shaw and his men. He was a great man, and I will do what I can to help you.' With that, he and I worked out a plan where he would help me recruit others to pose as the Negro soldiers. I would point out men who had the kind of features I was looking for, then he would go talk to them and introduce them to me. Soon I had my soldiers."

Gus continued, "I made some sketches and plasters of each head. Next I will pack them up and take them to my studio in Cornish."

My spirits fell, my eyes dropped to my lap, and I began to fumble with my beautiful ring.

"So you won't be staying here in Boston?"

Our times together were always so short and precious. This time in Boston had been especially joyous. But now once again, I would not see him for an indefinite period of time.

Gus immediately understood my change of mood. "My dear, I will make some trips to New York and stay at the Player's Club. Then we can have our time together. Look at me and know that I do not want to be away from you either."

I looked into his eyes, smiled, and said, "Sometimes I think I love you too much."

"And I you."

In 1885, Gus received a commission from the writer Henry Adams, who wanted a special memorial to his wife. She was a great artist in her own right, but she had struggled with depression and tragically ended her own life. Mr. Adams instructed Gus to make the memorial in such a way as to express the Buddhist belief in nirvana. The writer refused to see the preliminary clay model. He had his dear friend and artist, John La Farge approve the piece step by step.

The finished piece would be unveiled six years later in 1891. Visitors would whisper comments such as "Impressive," "Peaceful," and "Mysterious." When I would see it for the first time, it would bring tears to my eyes. It would be the most powerful piece of art I have ever seen. But there would be no mention of the mysterious lady in the sculpture.

Even in its early stages in 1885, the piece stirred many emotions for Gus. Once again, he felt torn between his love for me and his duty to his wife.

Gus turned to me and almost whispered, "My dear, as I have worked on this memorial, I have been reading about Buddhism and those beliefs. I am trying to see how my Christian beliefs do or do not fit in with thoughts of nirvana and enlightenment. I am still trying to make sense of it all."

He paused and knelt down in front of me. Looking deep into my eyes, he said, "I so want to marry you and be with you always. But I do not know how to do it without hurting everyone I know, especially Gussie. She is so frail and vulnerable that I do not think she would be able to recover if I left her."

It was true—Gussie was frail. She had been traveling to health spas and clinics, trying to find an answer to her deafness and other ailments. Homer was almost always with her.

He dropped his head into my lap. After a few moments, he asked, "Do you understand? You are my wife in spirit and heart, but I will have to remain legally married to Gussie. I know this hurts you as much as me, but always remember you alone are in my heart."

"Oh my dear, I do know and understand," I replied.

My heart was once again being torn apart because we could not be together as husband and wife. The church and society were unforgiving and unkind to people like us. To them, I was a sinner. Gus was also a sinner in the eyes of the church, but society "forgave" him, as long as he did not flaunt his affair. Little did they understand ours was not just an affair; it was a deep and enduring love.

When Gus returned to Cornish, Louis was living there too after returning from Toulouse. Louis's bouts of depression had gone unchanged. He now lived at Cornish and worked on projects for Gus at the studio there.

Louis pushed himself hard, taking little time to rest or eat. He kept to himself in the evenings, retiring to his room after supper and imbibing in too many glasses of wine or other drinks. In his worse times, he was known to climb atop a windmill, pull the ladder up, then sit there emptying his bottle of bourbon or wine.

When Louis was more capable, he helped Gus design an angel for the tomb of Anna Maria Smith, which would be erected at the Newport, Rhode Island, cemetery. This sculpture resembled the third angel originally planned for Morgan's tomb. The idea of taking his concept of the ethereal angel one step farther had never left Gus's mind.

I posed many hours, trying to capture the essence of this particular angel. I knew this was one of his most important pieces, and I was proud to be a part of it. As I posed, I relived happy memories from the forest in Sweden, or I thought of my love for Gus and how happy and proud of him I was.

The work was completed in 1886. However, Gus would have Louis put his signature on it later in 1887 to help quell any rumors about his affair with me.

CHAPTER 13

FOLLOWING THE HEART

1886

I was concerned about Gus's own health. Physicians had diagnosed Gus with neurasthenia because of his frequent complaints of stomach pains, indigestion, and exhaustion. The only prescribed cure was rest. Gus spent extra days resting at Cornish. He relied on Louis's expertise and talent to carry on the work in his stead.

Many days, Gus's melancholia would get the best of him. He would neither work nor play, but rather keep to himself. In time, though, he pulled himself out of his mood and got back into the studios as soon as possible.

Over the following months my life was busy, but I still tried to spend time with my family in Hoboken.

With each visit, however, I saw Nels grow weaker, refusing to get out of bed. It broke my heart to see my beloved uncle decline.

On one visit, we talked about his love for Ingrid and how she meant the world to him.

"She always encouraged and supported me," he said. "You know, she did not really want to leave Sweden, her family and friends. But she knew I could not fulfill my dream of having my own farm if I stayed there." A slight grin crossed his face. "When you have older brothers, they get the inheritance, even if they do not really want it."

He paused to let a coughing spell pass. "I achieved my dream when we bought this small but thriving place. And Ingrid has been happy working for Mr. and Mrs. Saint-Gaudens all these years, which gave you the opportunity to meet the love of your life."

We looked deeply into each other's eyes, smiled, and let our love flow between us. I bent down and rested my head on his chest for a moment. Once he fell asleep, I quietly slipped out of the room. Upon closing the door, I leaned against it and whispered a prayer to God for Nels to be healed.

Diana was Gus's newest commission. This sculpture was to be on top of Madison Square Garden as a weather vane. Gus would work on it with his dear friend Stanford. The two men sketched and planned. The greatest challenge was determining the right size and weight for *Diana* standing on top of an orb. They had to consider how well she would be seen, how well she could turn to follow the wind's changing directions, and how well she could withstand the strongest winds.

Gus came to my apartment to tell me about this newest endeavor. He said he wanted me to pose for *Diana*. The design was still in preliminary stages, but *Diana* would be nude, holding an arrow and bow pointing out. Flowing ribbons would trail behind her, as if the wind were blowing them. She would be standing on tiptoe with her other leg extended out.

"I will start with just your head, then do the rest of your body." He leaned toward me and looked straight into my eyes. "You understand that when I sketch the body, it will require you to be nude?" He continued looking and watching my facial expression. "Do you understand what that means?"

Many emotions flew through me. My mouth was dry, and my body felt cold.

"Yes, I think I understand."

He suddenly stood up and started to pace around the room. "I have given this a lot of thought. You have the perfect face and body, but I do not want this project to be too strenuous or difficult for you. My dearest, you are so innocent in so many ways. I do not want you to ever change that beautiful part of you."

We embraced, and he gently kissed me. We continued to hold each other, whispering words of love. Soon his hands were exploring my chest, gently opening up my dress with its many buttons, and soon he was kissing my breasts with such tenderness and gentleness.

Once my dress and underclothing had fallen away onto the floor, Gus slowly stepped away and whispered, "Yes, you are perfect to be Diana."

He took me by the hand and walked me to the full-length mirror in the bedroom, which I used everyday when dressing. I kept my eyes cast down, uncomfortable and embarrassed to see my body in such a manner.

"Davida, look at yourself. Look at the beautiful body God so graciously blessed you with."

I slowly looked up. I felt a mixture of discomfort and excitement. A warmth spread through my body, and I grew a little faint. Gus stood back as I continued to look at myself and feel a rush of passion. I turned to him.

"I will be your Diana," I said.

All I could think about was being with him. I trusted him, and I was flattered that he saw me as this Roman goddess of the hunt.

"Many people will not agree with your actions," he said, "and there may be harsh criticism and words said about you. Some might even respond with unkind or mean actions." He paused, then asked, "What about your mother and family? Are you worried about their reaction?"

I had been so caught up in the moment, I had not given any thought to these consequences or to how people, especially my mother, might respond. I turned away from the mirror, slipped on my shawl, and sat down on the bed. Soon my entire body was slightly shaking.

Gus sat on the bed next to me while saying, "There is much for you to think about, my sweet one, and I want you to make up your own mind. You do not have to decide now."

Gus must have read my thoughts. "I am sure that the idea of posing in the nude is scary or maybe embarrassing to you," he said. "Do not worry, my dear. What I do here is art. The human body is God's most beautiful and wondrous creation. Look into my eyes. Do you think I would ever ask anything of you that could bring you harm?"

I slowly shook my head; I did trust him.

Gus took my hand and affectionately stroked it. Then he spread my hand out on my thigh and traced the outline of my hand with his index finger. I felt a shiver run down my spine.

"Again, I would not do or ask anything of you that could hurt you. Artists such as myself live in a world uniquely different from the rest of the world. We do not live by rules of how a person should dress, walk, talk, or be. We see the beauty of the physical world in a spiritual way, different from conventional society."

He allowed me to take in his words with his hand still on mine. I gazed down at his small hand with its relatively short fingers. The fingernails were more square than rectangular. Underneath the powdery chalk, there was only a little hair and a few brown freckles scattered about. His hands emanated strength in a manner different from Papa's hands. These hands created beautiful art, from cameos to medallions to sculptures. For years as his model, I had been a part of this wonderful artist's creations. And now he was asking me to be a part of a very special creation unlike any other I had been a part of.

"When you invited me to pose for you for *Diana*, I had no idea what that really meant. I . . . I am not sure." I stammered while I tried to find the right words. I felt his hand grip mine tighter. "I will need to talk to Mother before I can say anymore."

I went to Hoboken to spend a couple of days with my family. But first, I visited Maria. I had to talk to her about *Diana*.

It was a joy to walk to Maria's house from the port, enjoying the late summer flowers and the trees in their fine greenery. Maria saw me coming and quickly opened the door. Her home was always bright, warm, and welcoming.

Maria went into the kitchen to get some tea while I sat in the large, comfortable blue winged chair, which was always my favorite. I listened to the ticking of the white porcelain clock sitting on the mantle. I breathed in the smells of lavender from a small bowl on the nearby table. The warmth of the sunrays filtering into the room calmed and relaxed me. Soon the gentle rattling of the teacups and saucers bouncing around on Maria's silver tray brought out of my reverie.

For the first time, I looked up at Maria with new eyes that had grown up. I was no longer the young girl who first met her on her way back from school so many years ago.

Maria too was different. I saw the knuckles on her long slender fingers looking large and red. Her skin was more wrinkled, and she had a slight shuffle to her gait. Were her shoulders more rounded? As I watched her pour the tea, I saw a slight shaking in her once ever-steady hands.

I suddenly realized ten years had gone by since we first met. In that time, I had selfishly ignored the changes in her physical body. In comparison, I noticed the changes of aging in my mother and aunt. But I always held Maria in a special light. To me, she was ageless because her spirit was ageless. The physical body, in time, will age, get sick, and someday die, but the spirit never dies.

Once we both had our tea, Maria asked me what I was so excited about. I told her everything about *Diana*. As always, she listened intently, not changing her expression. Her eyes never left mine, even when she raised her cup to her lips.

"I am fairly certain I want to pose for this piece," I said. "And if I do pose, I need your advice about how to tell my mother. I fear she would be against it and be most harsh with me. If she heard I were posing in the nude, I am scared she would forbid me from going back to the studio."

At last, Maria spoke. "I have some questions for you. They're not to embarrass or trouble you. They're intended to help you search your soul, so that whatever decision you make will be the right one for you.

Remember that society may look at things differently than you do. People may ridicule or even banish you for your decisions. But the only thing that ultimately matters is whether your decisions are right for your soul."

We looked into each other's eyes. I nervously smiled and slightly nodded.

"You and Mr. Saint-Gaudens have been lovers for some time now. Have you noticed any change in how people treat you?"

As soon as I shook my head, she continued.

"Has your mother or aunt treated you any differently?"

Again I shook my head.

"Do you think the human body is a marvelously beautiful creation of God?"

I nodded with a slight smile.

"And do you think the models, painters, and sculptors who create wondrous, magical, and almost-living works of art are sinful or bad?"

I shook my head.

"Of course not," she said. "You and I and everyone else in the world appreciate such masterpieces." She paused to sip her tea once more and take a bite of cookie. "So there's your answer on how to tell your mother."

I smiled at how simple she made it seem.

"Always be true to yourself, Davida, and know you are choosing to live as God wants you to live. That's all that matters."

I knew it was right to be the model for *Diana*. I silently prayed that my family would also come to accept this choice.

We spent the rest of the afternoon talking about my days in New York, the friends I had made, the other modeling jobs I had done, and of course my love for Gus and his projects.

"Have I told you about Mrs. Tutschek?" I asked. "Her name is Helen, and she lives just a few doors down from me. The two of you are so very much alike. You both have such a beautiful spirit about you."

Maria quickly replied, "Well, I would love to meet her someday. Perhaps you could invite her to come with you next time you visit."

"Yes, that would be wonderful. I often seek her advice when I cannot come to Hoboken. Or sometimes she and I just go shopping and seem to find lots of things to talk about."

As I stood to leave, I gave Maria a hug.

"Thank you," I said.

Despite my uplifting conversation with Maria, I felt the need to visit the forest before arriving at the farm Uncle Nels and Aunt Ingrid had bought so many years ago. The deeper into the woods I went, the more the tears spilled down my cheeks but also the more peaceful I felt. It was a warm day, and the sun's beams filtered through the tree limbs, which appeared to reach out and embrace the healing rays.

I sat down on the warm and welcoming soil and leaned against a tree. So many thoughts flitted in and out of my mind: "What am I to do? I want to be with Gus. I trust him. I agree with him that society sometimes puts too many restrictions on people. He is a renowned sculptor sought by the rich and famous. He is married. He has asked me to be his model for *Diana*, not his wife. Am I wrong to do this? What will people say? I do so love Gus, and I would do anything for him."

Suddenly I was overwhelmed by all these thoughts. I put my hands over my ears and screamed as loud as I could.

I opened my eyes and looked around, wondering if my screams had brought someone near. I sighed.

"Oh, Papa, I wish you were here. What am I to do?"

"Follow your heart."

I jumped up and turned around, expecting to see someone there.

"Follow your heart," the sweet and gentle voice repeated.

It seemed to sing in my ears. The light beams began to shimmer the colors of the rainbow as I heard those same words ringing softly in my ears, repeating over and over in my heart.

I instinctively knew Papa was there with me in the forest. It calmed my beating heart.

I heard his tenor voice saying, "I followed my heart so many years ago when I defied my family and married your mother. How I loved when your mother would blow a strand of hair off her forehead, how she would let out a little scream when something startled her, how she would have many conversations with herself, and how her eyes filled with tears when she said she loved me."

Did I love Gus? Or were my heart flutters just a young girl's signs of infatuation? He was married—a prosperous and respected member of the community. I was just a young woman who several years ago came to America. Then I shook my head as if to shake off these doubts. Of course, I loved Gus. I loved him with all my heart.

The light beams danced around me. With each passing moment, I felt more peaceful and assured.

"Thank you, Papa. I will follow my heart."

When I arrived at the farm, I went straight to see Uncle Nels. I was immediately concerned about his health. He was coughing more, and often the sputum had streaks of blood.

"I am fine," he would declare.

He still refused to go to the doctor. He looked pale and old. He still had his wonderful smile, but his coughing spells took a lot of energy out of him.

After supper, I told Mother, Ingrid, and Nels about my posing for *Diana* and what it meant to me. I even drew a very rough sketch of it. They listened without interruption as I talked. Then there was a long silence.

I could not tolerate how they looked at each other with furrowed brows and tight lips. "Well, I am doing this whether you approve or not," I finally said. I stood up to leave the room.

"Wait a minute. Albertina," Mother said. "You cannot expect us to just give you a quick response on such a serious subject. Please sit down and let's talk about it."

"I am sorry," I said, sitting back down. "I just want to do this so badly." I took another sip of tea, straightened my back, and looked them each in the eye. "You must understand that when I pose, I help create art. The human body is beautiful, and artists try to depict its beauty." I sounded like Gus. I smiled to myself, feeling very proud.

Nels spoke first. "My dear, you know I love you as if you were my own daughter. I do understand what you are saying and what you want. But it is different for us—to think about our own child and family member being drawn or sculpted in the nude."

I quickly interrupted him. "Yes, I will be in the nude, but no one will recognize the finished piece as me." I looked from Nels to Mother and asked, "What do you say, Mother? I will be doing this with or without your approval, but I would prefer to have your approval."

Mother looked down at her hands. "I can see your mind is made up. You are headstrong like your papa." She looked up into my eyes. "Yes, you have my approval, but only because I am trusting your judgment. I love you, and I only want what is best for you. But what I think is best may not be the right thing for you. Go ahead and tell Mr. Saint-Gaudens that you will do this."

The following morning, I awoke as soon as the sun began to rise. I found Mother in the kitchen. There was artistry in the way she opened the cupboard door and removed the teapot painted white with little pink roses. Those same hands then appeared to dance as each cup and saucer was placed on the little kitchen table. Her performance was complete when she poured the tea and handed me a cup.

Our private tea ceremony on that particular day would always be a special memory for me. I hoped I was even half as graceful and beautiful as she.

We sipped our tea until she interrupted the silence. "Now, regarding your feelings for Mr. Saint-Gaudens: Do you understand that you are treading in very dangerous and turbulent waters? He is a married man and has a high position in society. His wife is strong-willed and could cause you great pain. You are only twenty-five years old, compared to Mr. Saint-Gaudens, who must be fifteen or twenty years older than you. Have you considered that he might just be attracted to your youth and beauty, not to the essence of who you are? I do not want to see you hurt."

I knew Mother's words made sense, but I did not want to be rational or consider consequences.

"He has professed a love, or feelings, for me. And I have seen and overheard things to make me believe he is not happy in his marriage with Mrs. Saint-Gaudens. I just want to be with him and please him. I am happiest when I am with him. That is what is in my heart."

We quietly sipped our tea and looked into each other's eyes. I put my cup down and started to aimlessly stir the remaining tea. The dark liquid swirled. It seemed to mimic what I was feeling.

Again, I knew I should be rational about being in a relationship with a married man. But that meant entering a darkness of not seeing Gus every day. My emotions went between happiness, fear, sadness, and peace.

I put my spoon down and confided, "Mother, I have often gone to the forest, and various fairies have visited me. The fairies tell me I should follow my heart. And Mother, you know Papa believed in the fairies. It is him talking to me through the magical beings of the forest."

Mother's eyes shimmered. "Oh, my dear, you are in love. But I do worry for you. Please know I am here for you as you follow your heart— but please be careful." Mother tucked a wisp of hair behind her ear. "I am glad you seek guidance and advice from the mysterious and wondrous forest creatures, but also from the very human and rational Maria!"

Mother and I embraced one another. Soon I felt her tears dampening my cheek. We stood there for a long time and rocked in each other's arms.

I whispered, "I love you, Mother. I pray that my love for Gus is as strong as the love you and Papa had."

That day, I learned that if I stayed true to my being, followed my heart, and listened to God's words through Papa and the magical beings of the forest, I will have made the right decision.

CHAPTER 14

Diana

1887

Gus was pacing around the studio when I entered through the small door. His brow was furrowed, and he appeared to be muttering to himself while he ran his right hand through his wavy red hair. Upon hearing the door open, he turned and came over to me. He did not say anything but looked intently into my eyes.

"I am sorry I am late," I said. I curtsied and kept my eyes cast down, fearful he was angry with me.

Gus's words came out all at once. "It has been several days since we last talked. I was worried I had overwhelmed you. Are you okay? Have you given more thought to being the model for *Diana?* Will you do it?"

I slowly looked up into his eyes, which were searching for an answer. I so wanted to tell him about the magic of the forest and "seeing" my papa, but I merely nodded my head. I whispered, "Yes."

"Oh, my dear—you don't know how happy and relieved I am! You will not regret this. I promise." He wiped some perspiration from his forehead, then put his monogrammed handkerchief into his side pants pocket. "I will take good care of you. Only Louis or I will do the majority of the work, so you need not worry about the other workers seeing you." He took my chin and lifted my face toward him. "Someday you will be famous."

The first few days involved many poses of just my head, some with my hair loose and flowing, then some with it pulled back at the nape of the neck. Finally Gus decided on a tight bun pulled to the middle of my head. I posed, turning at various angles.

"Now, turn your head just slightly up a little more." "Move your eyes more this way." "Tighten your jaw." "Relax your neck." "Smile." "Look sad." And so the commands continued.

After long hours of instructions, Gus said, "Oh, that is perfect! Now just hold that for a minute."

To do the bust of my head, Gus wanted me to remove my upper clothing and just wrap my shawl around me.

"I must include your beautiful shoulders and neck," he explained.

Shaking a little, I stepped into the small area I used as a dressing room. The air was thick, and I had trouble catching my breath. I leaned against one wall while I slowly unlaced my bodice, removed my arms from the sleeves, and let the bodice fall to the floor.

I felt the warm air touch my breasts, which was exciting and scary. I touched my breasts and closed my eyes, dreaming about the first time Gus touched my breasts and we made love.

With a deep breath, I wrapped the shawl around my shoulders and returned to posing. My breasts were not exposed at first, but in time I was comfortable letting the shawl drop down a little. I was actually excited to show my chest and the tops of my breasts to Gus.

With each day, I became more comfortable disrobing. Louis was often in the studio too, but he was so absorbed in his projects that I do not think he even saw me. I became aware of new feelings and sensations in these intimate moments with Gus.

"You are so beautiful, Davida. Do you know that?" he asked.

I shook my head and lowered my eyes, suddenly feeling vulnerable and even a little ashamed. His compliments were flattering—so why was I experiencing such new feelings? My cheeks got warm, and little beads of sweat formed on my forehead.

"Thank you, Gus."

Two weeks later on a Monday morning, Louis greeted me with a cup of tea.

"Today we will do a few sketches of your upper body."

He paused. I nodded casually while I sipped my tea.

"There will be no one here except you and me," he added, watching for my reaction.

My head jerked up, and I searched Louis's eyes. "Where is Gus? Why won't he be here?" My voice trembled at the thought of his absence—and at the thought of showing my body alone here with Louis.

"He left for Boston early Saturday morning for an emergency meeting. He will be back tomorrow." Louis shuffled his feet and spoke quietly and respectfully. "Just as before, please remove your upper clothing, then wrap this shawl around your shoulders before you come out."

I went to the dressing area and removed my clothing. I leaned against the wall and quietly whispered to myself: "I can do this. Louis is Gus's brother, an artist in his own right. To him, I am nothing more than a model."

A gentle knocking at the door pulled out of my reverie. "Miss Clark, are you ready?"

I stepped out of the room, clutching the shawl around me. Louis guided me to a small platform and explained in a low tone of how I would stand with my arms outstretched as if I were shooting an arrow.

"Do you think you can do this without the shawl around you?"

Always the kind man, he gently helped me slip the shawl down, exposing my breasts with nipples hard and extended.

Seeing as I had never held a bow and arrow, I did the best I could as I posed.

"Your arms need to be higher," Louis instructed. "Pull your right arm straight back." "Extend your left arm out more." "Turn your head." "Raise your chin." "Now look straight ahead."

Those were the words I heard several times as I tried to capture the correct look. My arms and shoulders were aching. I finally had to ask Louis for a break.

"Oh my dear, I am so sorry. Of course, please sit down and rest." He scurried over to his worktable, grabbed my shawl, and put it around my shoulders. "Perhaps a cup of tea would be nice? Don't you agree" He quickly went across the studio room and poured two cups of tea.

"Louis, you are so kind. I am still not used to standing so long without any movement."

I tightened the shawl, drank the tea, and set my head against the back of the chair. With my eyes closed, I began to imagine a real bow and arrow in my hands. I pictured stretching the string and pulling the arrow, steadily holding my left arm straight and tight. I kept reimagining that pose. I relived a day when Papa and I were out in the woods. He had shot a boar with such precision right into its neck that the large animal fell quickly to the ground with one loud squeal of pain.

Then I heard Louis asking, "Are you ready, my dear? We should continue while the light coming into the room is still bright."

Louis and I continued until noon. After my visualization of the bow, I was relieved that I was finally able to capture the pose he wanted.

"You are doing such a beautiful job now," he said. "You are imitating what a bow marksman look like. Even your face shows the determination of a hunter ready to make her kill."

At the end of the day, I rushed home not knowing if Gus might come later that day or evening. I undressed, loosening the laces of my bodice, and I removed the pins holding my hair in a tight bun. I shook my head and pulled my fingers through my long locks, letting my naturally curly hair fly in every direction. I enjoyed the freedom of my hair as it was meant to be.

I murmured to myself, "God would give us all straight hair if He meant for it to always be hidden in a bun."

I then stretched out on the bed to rest awhile.

Next thing I knew, I was surprised to awaken to the clock chiming seven times, the birds chirping outside my window, and the bright sun shining through my lace curtains. I had slept through the whole night.

In early April I went to see my beloved uncle Nels—who was like a father to me—one last time. Mother had called and said he was declining rapidly. He had stopped eating for the last few days.

"I think he is hanging on just to see you, Albertina," she said.

My dear uncle was so thin and frail. I quietly sat next to his bed and waited for him to open his eyes. We briefly talked about his love for Ingrid and how she meant the world to him.

I whispered in his ear, "Rest now. We can talk more later."

Nels shook his head and took my hand. His last words to me were, *"Mitt kära barn, ta hand om Ingrid åt mig! Hon kommer att behöva Dig nu mer än någonsin."* Or, "My dear child, take care of Ingrid for me! She will need you more now than ever."

That night, he passed away in his sleep. Ingrid was as well prepared as she could be.

The day after the funeral, we three women sat around the kitchen table, drank our morning tea, and discussed plans for the future. Ingrid wanted to keep the farm, though Uncle Nels had encouraged her to sell it, knowing it would be too much for her and Mother to run alone.

"Ingrid," I said, "I know how much the farm means to you. And I know that you and Mother have been doing all the work for several months now. But you work for Mrs. Saint-Gaudens, and Mother works at the inn. I fear it is just too much for you both."

My aunt wiped some tears and nodded. "Nels and I had many discussions about the farm. He knew it would be best for me to sell it after he was gone. It is such a hard thing to even think about now." She grew very quiet and looked around the kitchen. "Everywhere I look, I see my beloved Nels. There is his coat hanging on the wall, ready for him to grab before going outside."

She went to the coat and nestled her face in it, taking in all the smells. After a few minutes, we took her upstairs to rest.

Just before closing her eyes, she turned to me and asked, "Will you come with me to the bank tomorrow? I do not know how to talk business."

I brushed her hair off her forehead. "How about we wait a week? I will ask Maria to come with us. She is even better at understanding business."

"Bless you my child. That is a good idea."

In a month's time, the farm sold. Mother and Ingrid moved into a boarding house a few blocks from me in the city. It was a tumultuous time of emotions and change. The last day at the farm, I went to the nearby woods and prayed for strength and guidance.

Ingrid continued to work as the housekeeper for the Saint-Gaudens household, and Mother found work as a cook at a hotel in Manhattan. She did not want to leave her position at Whispering Pines Inn, where she had worked for so long, but she knew it was best to live and work in the same area. Maria understood Mother's situation and was most gracious but sad to let her favorite employee go.

I went to see Maria as often as I could. It saddened my heart to see her living alone and declining in health. But she would not hear of leaving her home when I offered for her to come and stay with me.

CHAPTER 15

GOD-LIKE SCULPTOR

1887–88

The year of 1887 ended with the unveiling of *The Puritan* at Stearns Square in Springfield, Massachusetts, on November 24—six years after it was first commissioned. There was no parade or brass band. The townspeople were very pleased with the statue, though, and applauded Gus for his outstanding work.

Standing Lincoln was unveiled in Chicago that same year. Gus had done a lot of research before designing the magnificent statue. He had an artist friend send him some plaster casts of Lincoln's hands and face, and he recruited the former president's tailor to get one of his suits. Everything was as authentic as possible, and with Gus's talent as a sculptor, it all came together in *Standing Lincoln*. In years to come, it would be compared to the famous Lincoln Memorial in Washington, DC. Critics loved it, and the people of Illinois welcomed it with great praise and admiration.

I traveled to Chicago on my own and stood among the crowd to watch the unveiling. I watched Gussie and Gus sitting together on the dais, but this time their son, Homer, was with them. My heart ached at the sight, and I fought back my envy. "Just once, *I* want to be proudly standing next to him at an unveiling," I thought. That was a dream that would never come true.

It was easy to be just another face in the crowds because there were thousands of people in attendance. The wind was cold and threatening rain, so I held my hat down over my face and kept my umbrella close.

The speeches were long and boring, but once the gun salute fired, there was a lot of commotion from a horse near the statue. He reared up on his hind legs and tried to escape with the buggy still filled with two ladies, who were tossed about. Otherwise, the unveiling was a very special event and applauded by the press.

Later, Gus and I talked and laughed about the fiasco with the horse and the boring speeches. Then I grabbed his strong hands and held them to my cheek.

"I felt so a part of the Lincoln statue because of my happy memories when we spent time together in Chicago," I said. "Gus, I love you with all my heart. I am so proud of your statue. Lincoln was such a great man, and your work is beautiful."

When Gus was not working at his four studios, meeting with prospective customers, working with Stanford, or spending time in Cornish, he was teaching at the Art Students League. He was well liked by the students, who found him to be kind, sometimes moody, and very gifted. He enjoyed working with the students, as it recalled his own days of learning so many years ago.

When Gus could take time away from his busy schedule, he would come to my apartment. We treasured our time together. I would fix some traditional Swedish meals, which he enjoyed. He especially liked my cabbage rolls made with beef, rice, and my mother's special tomato sauce. After supper, we would curl up together and take turns reading to each other. It gave me a chance to improve my ability to read in English and pronounce words correctly.

One of Gus's favorite books was *New Arabian Nights* by Robert Louis Stevenson, which was a collection of short stories. The year before, Gus's good friend Will Low had arranged for Gus to meet Mr. Stevenson. Gus was so honored and thrilled. A deep friendship between the two men developed.

In honor of his new friend, Gus began to work on a small bronze relief, a plaque of Stevenson sitting on a couch with a quill in his hand. The plaque was framed with Scottish heather and Samoan hibiscus interwoven along the top and sides. The flowers had great significance for the famous writer, who was born in Edinburgh and lived in the South Pacific.

Gus told me how they became friends and how he admired Stevenson's writings and life choices. He could understand how Stevenson had fallen in love with his wife, Fanny, while she was still married to her first husband.

"His health has never been good, though," Gus said. "Since childhood, he has had respiratory problems, especially in cool, damp climates. I am worried about him." He closed the open book we had been reading. "Did I tell you Stevenson gave me the greatest compliment one day when in a letter he called me 'the God-like Sculptor'? He gave me the name after hearing a poem by Ralph Waldo Emerson."

The friendship would last until Stevenson's untimely death in 1894. Gus's dream to truly honor Stevenson would became a reality in 1904, when he unveiled his third and final version of the bronze plaque. It showed his friend again reclined on a couch, with his hands and head in more detail. It also included the words from the poem *Songs of Travel.* It was a masterpiece that was hung in Saint Giles' Church, Edinburgh.

Soon after the new year had begun and we were at the studio, Gus said, "I have such a great and burning desire to create a magnificent piece of sculpture that will capture the perfect ethereal female."

He was standing and looking upward. To my eyes, he was looking at just the same old ceiling. But his eyes were aglow with vision.

"An airy, mystical, delicate being," he continued. "An angel that is refined—more than beautiful." He turned to me and asked, "Do you know what I mean? I know I probably sound crazy."

I slowly shook my head but encouraged him to keep telling me more.

"The Morgan angels, the angel for Mrs. Smith's tomb, and those for

Mr. Vanderbilt's mantle are good examples, but not quite what I am envisioning."

He went to his table and started sketching, muttering a few words I did not understand. After a few minutes, he began to hum his favorite piece of music from Beethoven's Fifth Symphony. He soon burst into full singing. He was in a very special state of mind as his hands continued to sketch and sketch some more.

"Look at this," he said, showing his drawing. "Do you see now what I am trying to capture?"

I nodded and smiled. I could see an angelic face so similar to the face of the angel for the Anna Maria Smith tomb.

"I want you to pose for me. You are the only one who can do it."

As I posed, he again explained his concept of the ethereal woman, who was mystical, beautiful, spiritual, delicate yet strong, heavenly, and loving. She was perfection of womanhood.

I tried to capture the look of sweetness, love, and strength by thinking of my mother, whom I saw as this ethereal woman Gus described. I remembered certain expressions on her face, especially when she was thinking of Papa or when she was sitting in our garden in Sweden and staring off into the woods.

Gus often draped a muslin cloth over me, working the folds until they were perfect. He wrapped a garland of flowers around my waist and set a wreath of flowers atop my hair, which was parted in the middle and gently swept to each side in waves. As he instructed, I stretched my arms above my head and turned my head slightly down and to the right.

Once completed a year later, the angel stood in a hollow niche with her arms stretched high above her head, holding a tablet. Her wings curved upward, and she wore a flowing gown that barely covered her feet. On her head was a crown of flowers, and a garland of flowers was around her waist. Her facial expression was one of love, peace, and harmony.

This was the start of a long, meaningful, and special journey we shared. When completed in 1898, the piece would be called *Amor Caritas*.

CHAPTER 16

NEW BIRTH

1889

In late February 1889, I awoke to such nausea I wondered if I had influenza. The nausea continued only in the mornings for several days, then I realized I had not had my menstrual period last month. Despite the bitter cold and large amount of snow on the ground, I went to Hoboken to see Maria the following month.

After I described how my health had been the past several weeks, Maria nodded and said, "My dear, it appears to me that you are about to become a mother."

"No, no, no, no," I kept repeating. "I cannot have a baby. What will this do to Gus's career and his family?"

I took out the white lacey handkerchief Gus had bought for me. I had not seen Gus for a few weeks because he was spending more time at his studios. He had several smaller projects to complete and also prepare for a trip to Paris in June. Holding the handkerchief made me feel close to him.

"Maria, what should I do?"

"First of all, if you were married, would you want to keep the baby?" When she acknowledged my nodding head, she went on. "Then keep the baby and raise the little darling with all your love. I don't mean to sound harsh, but Gus will have to handle his career and family. He always knew there was a chance something like this might happen. After all, he did pursue you because of his love for you."

We sat in silence for a while. I became lost in my thoughts about being a mother. I did want this baby. There was no doubt about that. I smiled as I tried to imagine Gus and myself adoring a child—*our* child.

But then my happiness was interrupted as I thought about how Mother and Ingrid would respond. I let out a groan and dropped my head into my hands.

"Oh dear God, how do I tell my mother and aunt?"

Maria stood up and walked over to me. She put her arms around me and rested her head on top of mine.

"None of this will be easy at first, but it'll all be fine in the end. Just remember everything you've been through these past years since meeting and working for Gus. You've followed your heart and held your head up high. And that's what you'll have to do again."

I spent the night at Maria's. After more discussions, laughter, and tears, I was ready to face my next challenge.

On the following Sunday, I greeted my mother and aunt as they walked in the front door after church. They could see in my eyes and demeanor that something was wrong.

We sat in the parlor, and they quietly listened as I told of my pregnancy. They both surprised me with their acceptance and understanding.

"We are not surprised, Albertina," Mother said. "We are only surprised it did not happen sooner."

They glanced at each other, then came over to me. We stood together in an embrace.

"We are here for you and will help you in any way we can," Ingrid said. She let out a long sigh and went on, "There might be a lot of gossip, especially if Mrs. Saint-Gaudens finds out."

Mother quickly added, "You must tell Mr. Saint-Gaudens as soon as possible. You need to know if he will stand beside you, or if he will regretfully leave your relationship."

I did not want to take Gus away from his work, but I had to tell him about the pregnancy. Louis delivered a note to him simply saying it was very important that I see him as soon as possible.

I waited at the train station with butterflies in my stomach. It took Louis a few days to personally give Gus my note, who then sent me a telegram saying, "I will be arriving on the one o'clock train." I paced the platform and kept straightening my dress and adjusting my hat. I wanted to look the very best for him and not draw attention to what I thought was my bulging stomach. I was now four months along.

He stepped from the train and immediately glanced around in search of me. I waved, smiled nervously, then ran up to him. I threw my arms around his neck and held on to him with all my love and strength.

"My dear, I am glad to see you too, but you are taking the air right out of me!" He laughed. Then he held me at arm's length and searched my eyes. "Something has happened. I can see it in your eyes. Are you okay? Is it your mother or your aunt?"

His questions came so quickly that all I could do was shake my head. "No. Everything is fine. Let's go home, and we can talk then."

The ride seemed unusually long. We entered my small apartment, welcoming its warmth and privacy. As I took off my wrap, he took me into his arms.

"Now, tell me what has taken the lovely smile from your face."

"Come—let's sit down, and I will tell you everything."

He listened intently, never taking his eyes off me as I told him about the pregnancy and what had transpired the past four months.

I concluded, "Now, if you want to leave and never return, I will not stop you. I do not want to be the cause of your career suffering. I love you too much to do that."

We sat quietly for what seemed an eternity. My heart was pounding. Although I knew he loved me, I also knew how much his career meant to him. Finally, he stood up, walked to the window, then turned back to me.

"Davida, I know how hard this must be for you. I love you with all my heart, and I will always be here for you." He paused and turned back toward the window for what seemed a very long time. "I need some time to think about all of this. I need to plan for how this could affect my family, my career. You do understand, don't you?"

I nodded and dreaded hearing his next words.

"I need to go away for a while and think about all of this. There is an exposition in Paris coming up, so I will book passage to it. My leaving won't raise any suspicion or be a surprise to anyone." He stroked his beard. He asked, "How are you feeling? Are you all right?"

I nodded. "Yes, I feel fine now."

"Again, I hope you understand my need to be away for a while. I must think what is best for you as well as for me. You do understand, don't you?"

I smiled and said, "Of course I do. There are a lot of things to decide."

There was no further discussion about the pregnancy during the weekend he stayed with me. We could feel the tension and uncertainty, but there was no doubt about our love for each other. We played games, read to each other, took walks, and made love with the same passion.

Two weeks later, Gus sailed to France.

He was in Paris for a short time, where he took a room at a hotel. He had confided only in his friend Paul Bion about this short visit.

Upon his return, he shared with me that he had spent many hours thinking how best to handle the new situation.

"I considered immediately leaving Gussie, filing for divorce, and marrying you. But I am fearful of the affect it might have on Gussie, who is not a strong woman. In so many ways, she is very frail, which she hides with her austere personality. And I know how people talk and can be so judgmental. I worry that a divorce and remarriage might bring my successful career to ruin in a short time."

I listened intently to his every word, watched his face and body movements. He often wiped his forehead and blew his nose as he paced up and down. My heart was ripping apart for him, but I did not know what to do but to listen and sit quietly.

He suddenly turned, sat down next to me, and tilted my head to look into his eyes. "And you, my dear one, I do not want to hurt you. I so wish we could just run off and marry and raise our child together, but that is not to be. I have a responsibility to my son, Homer, as well as my new child. You do understand, don't you?"

I slowly moved my head while my eyes filled with tears. "I do understand, my love. Whatever decision you have made I will honor."

The minutes ticked by as we looked into each other's eyes.

Finally he said, "I will not now or ever abandon you or our child. I will always be in your lives, just as I have been in your life for these many years. I am sure you understand that I cannot leave Gussie nor risk my career. The possible consequences are too great."

I had known deep in my heart that that would be his decision. I loved him too much to ask for anything less. He was an honorable man with a generous heart full of love for me—but also for Homer, Gussie, and his art.

"Can we go on as we have?" I asked. "Will you still come to see me when I am fat and lazy with child? The neighbors here already think you are my husband, who works as a traveling salesman, so nothing has to change except now we are going to have a beautiful baby."

Suddenly, he picked me up and twirled me around. We laughed and cried as he declared, "My *amor caritas*, see why I love you?"

I must say, the months of pregnancy were not always easy. But once the morning sickness passed and I felt rested, the joy of bringing a new baby into the world only increased. I proudly walked down the boulevards or rode the trains. When I could feel the baby move or kick inside me, I excitedly shared the moments with Mother, Aunt Ingrid, Maria, and, of course, Gus.

He smiled from ear to ear, saying, "I never got to do this when Gussie was pregnant with Homer. I am so happy and grateful I can share these moments with you."

Mother and I had many talks about bringing up a child.

"There are challenges," she said, "but there are more joys and happy moments to balance the difficult times. You must teach the baby with love how to behave. During the toddler years, you may have to use some tougher discipline, but always with love."

"Oh, Mother, I hope I can be half as good a mother as you have been to me."

We decided to have a midwife with Aunt Ingrid assisting to deliver the baby at home. Gus had the three of us move into the Grand Central Hotel in mid-September to keep us near the finest hospitals and doctors, if they should be needed.

On September 22, my first contraction came shortly after supper. Initially I did not know what it was, but more came within minutes.

Mother called out, "It has begun! Come—let us get you into bed. Ingrid, telephone the midwife to come right away."

My beautiful son with his dark hair arrived into the world crying at the top of his lungs. The midwife did not have to slap his tiny bottom. The ecstasy when my sweet child was placed upon my chest was overwhelming. I cried with tears of such joy and peace I had never felt before.

Gus arrived two days later. He held his son and stroked his head. It was such a happy moment watching the love of my life hold our new little angel. I had never been happier.

I quickly asked, "What shall we name him? I have a name in mind, but I want to hear your ideas first."

"Well, if you would not mind, I would like to name him Louis, after my brother whom I love so much."

I almost jumped from the bed. "Oh, perfect! That is the name I wanted also. I too love your brother and have a very special place in my heart for him. Do you have a middle name in mind?"

"Yes, I do, but I want to hear what name you would want."

"Well, I loved my father so much. Would it be okay if we named him Louis Gustaf?"

Gus drew a bit of a frown as he softly repeated the name. "It seems a little awkward, doesn't it? Louis Gustaf does not have a nice flow."

My heart sank a little when Gus suggested Louis Paul, after his father, whose middle name was Paul. But I did have to admit it had a nice ring to it. It rolled off the tongue much more easily.

Gus could only stay the one night because Homer's ninth birthday was coming up on the twenty-ninth. He had promised Gussie he would be back home for the birthday celebration, which was to be quite grand.

This was a scenario that would be repeated for many years. It was quite amazing that Augustus Saint-Gaudens's only two children would have birthdays within six days of each other. The two brothers would never meet, and I would never see Gussie again.

I loved being a mother and found myself wanting to be with Louis every minute. His dark hair had a little wave, his skin had a slight olive complexion, and his eyes turned from blue to hazel, just like Gus's. He ate well and quickly outgrew his baby fat. As a toddler, he was muscular but slim.

I would sit on the floor and help him build blocks or play with the Dalecarlian horse I had as a child. When he got tired, he would pick up his bunny rabbit Mother made for him. His thumb went into his mouth, and he would hold his rabbit with the other hand. I would hum "The Cradle Song" by Brahms while I rocked him to sleep.

From the time of Louis's birth, I referred to Gus as his papa. But one evening when Gus was visiting, Gus initiated a conversation after I put Louis to bed.

"My dearest, think about the confusion for our sweet son if he calls me Papa yet I do not live here. When he gets older, this will create more confusion for him."

At first I was angry and taken aback. "Well, if you would get a divorce so we could get married, then our son could freely call you Papa, and there would be no confusion."

My voice was harsh, my words were cruel and selfish, but they expressed my deepest feelings. I loved Gus so much. I hated being apart from him for even a minute. And I was jealous of the life he had that did not include our son and me.

The silence in the room was heavy. Gus looked at me with his eyes wide open and his jaw tightly set. He had never before seen me angry and questioning his behavior. He looked down at the floor and struck his knees with his fists.

After a few minutes, I sat down next to Gus and repeated several times, "I am so sorry, my beloved."

He replied ever so gently, "I understand that none of this is easy for you. But I have to think about my other family and my career. I could lose commissions and be ostracized, which is not something I can afford for the sake of my finances nor for the sake my soul."

"I am sorry I said those words. I do understand the difficult situation you are in, and I do not want to be an obstacle to your career or your other family." I tried not to cry, but the tears flowed freely, releasing many emotions I had been holding in. "It is just that I love you, and I want Louis to know who his father is."

Gus cupped my face, lifting it up toward his. "Come sit on my lap so I can hold you close."

We kissed and embraced. I felt myself soar into another dimension, floating where there was nothing but love.

Later that day, we decided that Louis would call Gus Papa while we were together in private. But if we were in public and met someone who knew him as Augustus Saint-Gaudens, then we would introduce Louis as his nephew. I was concerned that this would confuse Louis, but I was elated that Gus would be Papa—even if only in privacy. I so wanted Louis to love and know his father, as I did mine.

I later learned that what we want for our children might not always come to fruition.

Chapter 17

Novy

1890–92

After the birth of Louis, I continued to model for *Diana*, exposing more and more of my body. With each passing day, it became easier for me to stand in the nude. I knew I was contributing to a great work of art that was important to Gus, and that was all I cared about. I wanted to do anything to help him be successful and happy.

This *Diana* assignment was much more demanding on my body than any other project. To capture the stance of *Diana* standing on top of a ball, Gus placed two ladders in such a way that I was braced between them. Still, the tiptoe position was quite painful. During rest periods, which needed to occur more and more frequently, I had to massage the arch of my foot.

Then after one particularly long day at the studio, Gus took me aside and whispered, "My sweet darling, I must ask you to trust me in what I am about to say."

I wiped perspiration from my face and pulled a few loose strands away. I nodded. "Yes. I completely trust you, so please know you can say anything you need to."

"Well, I think this particular project is too much for you. We have to take too many breaks, and your exhaustion shows in your entire body, right down to your dainty feet."

He stopped to search my face. I am sure he saw some confusion and disappointment.

"I know of another model," he continued. "Her name is Julia Baird, and most people call her Dudie. She is free to help me finish this project. She has the youthful stamina for this kind of posing. I will be incorporating much of the sketching and preliminary casts of you with whatever sketches and molds I make with her."

I nodded again. I felt an array of emotions—disappointment, anger, jealousy, then relief. It was true—I was coming home exhausted every afternoon and knew I was taking more breaks than Gus wished. I was nearly thirty. My youthful body had changed after having a child, and my energy and endurance had ebbed. Plus, I still had responsibility with our little son and needed several days off to be with him.

With Julia now taking my place, I stayed home for the next two weeks and only visited the studio twice to have lunch with Gus. I was also quite curious to meet Julia after I learned more about her. She was only seventeen years old, and her father's untimely death had propelled her into the modeling business. In the years to follow, she would pose for many other noted sculptors and artists. She was beautiful and had a nice figure. I had to admit, I was a little envious because she was posing instead of me.

During one of my visits, I met Julia. Gus quickly interrupted our brief introduction when he said, "Time to get back to work."

I never saw her again, nor did I tell Gus about my jealousy. After all, I knew it was my weakness to hold certain poses for a long time that caused Gus to have Julia take my place.

One day a year later, I was walking toward the studio, marveling as the snow slowly melted under the bright sunshine. The landscape was one of magic and splendor. I stopped once and lifted my head upward, remembering my home in Stora Blåsjön.

When I entered the studio, Gus was standing by the *Diana* statue in plaster, looking at it with intensity. He was humming and stroking his beard, occasionally muttering under his breath. I stood quietly nearby, trying to catch his words. I knew this was an important time for him. I thought, "God is speaking to him."

After what seemed a very long time, Gus suddenly turned and looked at me. "You are late! I was beginning to worry."

He walked toward me with his arms outstretched. I welcomed the warmth of his embrace, savoring the moment. His white shirt was stiffly starched and felt rough against my cheek, but I did not care. I was in his arms. Nothing else mattered.

"My sweet one, I have just a few finishing touches I want to do on *Diana*. There is something about the face that is not quite right. Diana was the goddess of the hunt, the moon, and childbirth in Roman mythology. You love the forests. Go there in your mind, and see yourself as the goddess of all the animals and the forest."

He brought a stool over and directed me to sit. He moved my head around, then walked over to the sculpture.

"Now, my beautiful Davida, become the goddess of the woods and the moon."

At first my mind was focused on the word *goddess*, to which I could not relate. But I closed my eyes for a few minutes, letting my imaginary thoughts flow through me. I soon saw myself standing in the woods— trees gracing the landscape, a warm shaft of sun shining on me like a spotlight, and a deer at my side. Everything was peaceful and loving.

My dreamlike state was interrupted by the words, "Perfect. Perfect. I have it! I have the face of *Diana*." Gus kissed me on the cheek and said, "Why don't we go for lunch at the eatery around the corner to celebrate?"

I stood by Gus and gazed at the completed mold of *Diana*. The head was of me, and the youthful body was Dudie's. I could see the beauty Gus had captured. I marveled at the attention to detail.

"*Diana* represents the woman's body as God intended," he said. "She shows strength, determination, yet gentleness."

I agreed. Gus truly had captured the essence of his vision of a strong and beautiful woman.

Gus was very proud of his work, yet he knew he and Stanford still had to perfect the platform on which she would stand. She needed to turn in the strong winds three hundred feet in the air, atop Madison Square Garden.

On September 28, 1891, *Diana* was finally hoisted atop the thirty-two-story-high building. Immediately, Gus and Stanford both saw that the figure was too large, standing eighteen feet tall and weighing eighteen hundred pounds. The statue did not turn smoothly with the winds, as any weather vane should.

Gus had to work through many issues. He had to balance the statue on the round globe, upon which *Diana* stood on her left toe. He also had to create balance with the long ribbons that swirled around her nude body and swept outward, as if blowing in the wind. Not to mention, he had to deal with the people who objected to a nude body made of copper and demanded that clothing be added.

The statue was removed in 1892, later to be put on exhibit at the 1893 World's Columbian Exposition. In November 1893, the second *Diana* was hoisted atop Madison Square Garden. She stood only thirteen feet tall and was lighter, so it moved with the winds of New York City.

As a weather vane, there was no other one like it. With the sun's rays glancing off it, the gilded statue could be seen from as far away as New Jersey.

It was also the first time one of Thomas Edison's light bulbs was publicly used. Edison placed some 6,600 light bulbs around Madison Square Garden and another 1,400 on the tower, with an additional ten giant lights aimed at the statue. It was the first statue in history to be lit by electricity.

At some point the ribbons flowing from her body blew off during a windstorm and were not replaced. The beautiful statue had to be bolted down, which prevented it from turning. It was no longer the weather vane Gus had envisioned. But it was still a masterful piece of art.

In 1891, Gus bought the Cornish estate they had rented for several years. He named it Aspet in honor of his father's hometown. Gus converted the barn into a studio, though he continued to keep the other studios in New York City.

That same year, the lease on their Washington Place apartment ended, and the family moved to an apartment at Fifty-One West Forty-Fifth Street. Gus found Aspet's climate and scenery much more relaxing and much healthier than Manhattan's busyness and congestion. He split his time between New York and Cornish, but he stayed at Aspet often enough to create the image of he and Gussie as a happily married couple.

In early 1892, while working on the second *Diana*, Gus bought a home for Louis and me in the Noroton Heights neighborhood of Darien, Connecticut.

"Now that we have a child," he said, "you need a proper home in which to raise him."

The white clapboard home had a delightful wraparound porch and a large yard. The town had a school, shops, and beautiful neighbor-hoods. The New Haven railroad went right though Noroton. Soon after the Civil War ended, Noroton had seen a large building boom of vacation homes for the wealthy New Yorkers to escape to in the summer. There was a trolley connecting the town's streets, which Louis loved to ride.

On warm sunny days, Louis and I would walk around town, often stopping for a dish of ice cream. Sometimes we would go up the hill from town and walk among the hickory and walnut trees, which were surrounded by bushes of varying types. I still missed the tall pines and the open areas filled with pine needles, leaves, and boulders of New Jersey. But these woods in Connecticut had a beauty as well.

I tried to teach Louis about the magical beings that often lived in the woods. His eyes would get big and look for such creatures.

"I do not see any, Mama. Why can't I see them?"

"Sometimes they do not want anyone to know they are here. But they are there. They will keep us safe."

When Gus would visit, we would stroll hand in hand with Louis, as would any married couple in love with a child. I savored these times because we did not have to hide or worry about someone recognizing us. Neighbors were told the same story, that Gus was a traveling salesman often on the road.

One summer day, Gus surprised us with a weeklong visit to our home in Darien.

"Gussie and Homer are gone," he said, "and things are going well at the studio. I am free to spend time with you." His face was aglow, and he looked well rested for the first time in a long while.

Holding Louis on his knee, Gus ran his fingers through his son's thick hair. "I think I would like to make a bronze medallion of my Novy."

Novy was a new nickname Gus called Louis. I asked him about the name.

"When I was a young man in Paris," Gus explained, "I was sitting at one of the many cafés, enjoying a glass of wine and watching people go by. An elderly couple came to my table and asked if they could join me, seeing as there was no other table available. Of course, I welcomed their company. We talked, laughed, and shared stories. They introduced themselves as Adolph and Martina Novy on vacation from Czechoslovakia. They were very affectionate, and there was definitely love in their eyes. I knew then that I wanted that kind of a relationship with my wife. It turns out *novy* means 'new,' and you and Louis are my new wife and son."

I loved the story. I could just see my Gus, young and handsome, graciously making friends with this couple.

"So, Novy," Gus asked, "what do you think of me making a bronze medallion of you?"

Louis looked up and said, "Papa, my name is Louis. Did you forget?"

Gus laughed and hugged Louis. "No, I did not forget your name. But I am going to call you by this very special name, only from me to you. Is that okay? Can I call you Novy?"

Soon we had Louis dressed up in his brown jacket and short pants with his hair combed, ready to pose.

"Now, you must sit very still," Gus told him. "You and your mama can play a game to see who can sit the quietest the longest. Whoever wins will get to pick out any toy they want."

It was a delightful time. Gus made many sketches, quickly tossing each sheet of paper down on the floor. After about an hour, Louis finally tired of the "game" and needed a nap.

"Well, I know Louis won that game," I said. "He sat so still, whereas I had to move many times before he did!" I laughed. "We shall have to go to the big city tomorrow and pick out a prize for the winner at the biggest toy store we can find."

We took Louis to FAO Schwarz. His little mouth smiled from ear to ear, and his eyes danced from one toy to the next. We walked around the big store many times until Gus and I both were quite exhausted.

I put my hand on Louis's shoulder, knelt down to his eye level, and said, "Let's go have some lunch. When we come back, you can pick out which toy you want. Okay?"

With that, we found a little restaurant around the corner, where we all enjoyed lunch, followed by some ice cream. After lunch, Louis finally chose a hand-painted wooden rocking horse. It was too big for us to bring home, so the store delivered it the next day. We set it up on our front porch. Louis would play on the horse while we sat in the white wicker chairs, enjoying our time together as a family. I often wondered if Louis imagined riding a horse in some distant lands while he rocked back and forth. I took a photograph of Louis on his horse with me on the porch. Then we took one of him with his mormor, Grandma Hultgren.

A few months later, Gus brought over the beautiful bronze relief medallion showing Louis's profile. On the left side is NOVY, and on the right M/DCCCXC/II. I was so thrilled to have such a wonderful piece of art of my son made by his papa.

CHAPTER 18

FAMILIES

1893–94

In 1893, Gus presented his proposal for a memorial statue of President Garfield to be displayed in Philadelphia. Garfield had been assassinated in 1881. One week, Gus was so busy he asked me to go to Philadelphia and sign some papers for him. I was quite nervous about it and thankful that one of Gus's workers accompanied me. I simply signed my name, *D. Clark*.

Uncle Louis often came over to my new home in Connecticut. He enjoyed playing with his namesake nephew. I loved to hear their laughter ring through the house while they played various games.

I said to Louis one day, "I hope you will have children of your own someday. You are so good to our little fellow."

Louis looked away wistfully and quietly said, "I do also."

Immediately, I reprimanded myself for speaking without thinking. I had completely forgotten he had been married once and his wife died in childbirth.

Louis must have sensed how I was punishing myself. He came and put his arm around me.

"It is okay, Davida. I forget things all the time. But yes, I do hope to marry again and have lots of little ones running around the house.

DAVIDA

And if I am lucky, I will have a wife as beautiful and kind as you."

I smiled and gave a short bow. "Oh, thank you, Louis. You are so kind." I reached up and gave him a kiss on the cheek.

After a long decline in health, Louis and Gus's father, Bernard, passed away in June of 1893. Gus was quite shaken by his death. He spent the good part of an evening pacing up and down the parlor, crying and bemoaning that he had not spent more time with his father.

I quietly listened and watched, knowing Gus needed to let go of so many layers of emotions. He had struggled with his father's second marriage. Gus thought the woman had been taking advantage of Bernard by spending his money and stepping out on him with other men. Gus also admitted he could not think of any other woman taking the place of his mother, whom he so adored.

Soon Gus put his energy and emotions into his work. He started sketching for a statue of General Sherman. Gus had completed a bust of the general in 1888. During the sittings, the two men had become well acquainted and grew to consider each other friends. Around the time he started sketching the Sherman statue, Gus also transported the original *Diana* to the World Columbian Exposition in Chicago as well as completed a commemorative medal and a statue of Christopher Columbus for the exposition.

These were busy but happy times, though Louis and I were not with Gus often. We wrote many letters back and forth, all of which I kept and treasured.

Louis loved to hear me tell stories about his grandfather Gustaf. He was curious about my life in Sweden and tried to learn some simple Swedish words. He did love my cooking, even though it was never as good as Ingrid's or Mother's. But he did not like rutabagas and lima beans, no matter how I tried to cover their taste.

From spring to fall, I would teach Louis how to plant and take care of different vegetables and flowers. Just as I did when I was his age, he learned how to furrow the small rows and how to add just the right number of seeds in each hole. He also learned the difference between a

124

weed and a plant—even the weeds that mimic the plants they are near.

In the summer, he would help me preserve some vegetables, make jams and pickles, and hoe the soil frequently, keeping it loose and able to absorb moisture. In the fall, I would show him how to separate and a dry seed for next year's planting. These were special times, when my heritage and childhood years came alive again.

When Gus was not busy, we did enjoy some short visits with him. One evening in December, all of us went to Madison Square Garden to watch *The Nutcracker Suite*. When we stepped out of the taxi, we each looked up at *Diana*. Gus and I always thought it was one of his finest works. Unfortunately, society was not ready for a naked woman to literally be in the spotlight on top of one of the finest buildings in New York City.

Louis was all dressed up in a blue velveteen suit and a lace-collared shirt. He was such a handsome little boy. I think he was a little overwhelmed with the crowds of people and all the finery of dress and jewels.

It was one of the few occasions when we were out in society as a family. If Gus were uncomfortable introducing me, he covered it well. Gus would look people in the eye and simply say, "I would like to introduce Miss Davida Clark." His manner conveyed a message that no more needed to be said.

I was more nervous than he was. I was not familiar with the way higher-class people talked and acted. I sensed disapproval in their eyes.

One person who greeted me warmly was Stanford White.

"How nice to see you again," Stanford exuberantly said. He bowed and kissed my hand as he looked up at me and winked. He still had a reputation for being quite the lady's man, flirting with most women in hopes of having a conquest that evening.

The other side of Stanford White was his wonderful talent at stone masonry. He created some of the most beautiful bases and pedestals upon which statues stood—Gus's included. His reputation as a respectable artist was without blemish.

Once we returned home after such an exciting evening, Gus asked Novy, "Did you like the show tonight?" Upon seeing his son nod, he went on, "Did you know I play the flute?"

Louis shook his head.

"No? Well, someday I will have to bring it with me and play some music for you and your mama. Would you like that?"

With wide eyes, Louis looked up at his papa and almost whispered, "Yes, sir."

"That's my boy. Perhaps now is the time for you to learn to play an instrument. The piano is a good one to start with. You can learn to read music that would be the same for any other instrument."

Gus instructed me to find a piano teacher and that he would pay all the expenses. A piano was delivered in the next few days.

It was a night filled with family happiness. I so wished we could have had more of them, but that was not to be our destiny.

CHAPTER 19

THE BASTARD

1895–96

Novy was beginning first grade and would be away most of the day. I often felt quite alone when he was gone. I missed just spending the day with him, reading and playing games.

Helen invited me over for tea one early afternoon. After exchanging pleasantries, she asked, "So now with Novy in school, how do you fill your day?"

I responded with some hesitation, "Well, I am busy baking most of the day and preparing for our evening suppers."

"My goodness—that sounds like a lot of food for just two people," she exclaimed. She smiled warmly at me. "Davida, it's not unusual for you to feel lonely. Do you remember when my little Frank went off to school? I was a little bit lonely but quickly filled my days spending time with you and other friends."

I nodded and wiped some tears. "I am lonely. I miss Novy, and I miss Gus. What am I to do?" I shook my head trying to imagine what a middle-aged model was to do with her life. "I cannot be the model I used to be, though Gus does have a project coming up for me. It is a statue he is doing for President Garfield."

Helen came over and sat next to me. "My dear, there's one significant difference in our lives. That is, I have a husband who lives with me in the same house every day. I so wish you had that with Gus. It would make your life so much easier." She patted my hand. "Davida, you are like a sister to me. I said that not to hurt you, and I'm sorry if I did." She went on, "You have had a most interesting life, and you are very talented in many ways. Just your cooking alone is a rare gift."

I shook my head, believing I was nothing but a model who had lost her beauty and youth.

"Now, just listen to me for a minute," Helen insisted. "You could write a book of Swedish recipes."

I looked up at her with surprise.

"Yes. You make these delicious meals and desserts, and other women would love to know how to make them too."

"Oh, I do not know. I do not think my cooking is nearly as good as Mother's or Aunt Ingrid's." I had to smile, though, as I thought about all the days we three spent in kitchens together.

"Fiddlesticks! Of course your cooking is as good. Tomorrow I will come over and help you get started. Okay?"

That night as I lay in bed, I began to envision what dear Helen was talking about. My mind began to race thinking about the many dishes and how to present them in a cookbook. In the morning, I greeted Helen with a big smile, and we began my new adventure.

When I told Gus about the recipe book, he was equally enthusiastic and said he would help me in any way he could.

I felt a new lease on life. A new purpose had opened up. I spent many days writing out my favorite recipes. I wrote them in longhand on paper, then Helen took them to her husband's office, where the recipes were typed on beautiful linen paper. I then put them in nicely bound books and distributed them to ladies in the neighborhood. I also made a very special booklet for Novy. I put it aside, trusting I would know the right time to give it to him.

Gus came to visit for my birthday in December 1895. I was celebrating my thirty-fourth year with the two people I loved the most,

Novy and Gus. We went to Delmonico's for supper, then to one of the Broadway theaters to see *The Great Diamond Robbery*. It was a delightful evening. Novy, at six years old, enjoyed the excitement of the play.

The next day Gus surprised me with a proposal. "Let's plan a trip for just the two of us. We will go wherever you want sometime in January."

I was so pleasantly surprised, and my excitement rose as I thought about spending uninterrupted time alone with my love. Then I suddenly thought, "What about Novy? I cannot just leave him."

"He is in school all day, then perhaps he can stay with Helen. I am sure she will not mind, and Novy loves her." His eyes were dancing with anticipation and planning. "Now, where would you like to go?"

I gasped and said, "I do not know. There are so many wonderful places I have only dreamed about."

After much planning and arranging, Gus and I spent a fun and romantic week in Washington, DC, where I had never been. It was an exciting city with so much history and so many government landmarks, including the Washington Monument, the Capitol Building, and the White House. Gus and I spent some time marveling at the bronze statue of Andrew Jackson. He sits astride his horse, which is reared back on his hind quarters. We both were very impressed at the sculptor's feat to create such a masterpiece.

We stayed at the Morrison-Clark Inn, a Victorian mansion built in 1864. It was very private, opulent, and within walking distance of most historic sites. Some days we just wanted to be alone together, spending quality time talking, recalling memories, and discussing our hopes and dreams. We made love. We laughed. We cried.

All too soon, our beautiful time together ended like a fairy-tale book. Gus had arranged for us to have an exclusive five-course meal in a private area in their dining room. The table had a bouquet of white roses, which Gus knew was my favorite flower. A violinist came and played a medley of music including Beethoven's Fifth Symphony.

We were enjoying a very specially prepared chocolate dessert when Gus reached in his pocket and handed me a small box with a red ribbon.

"For you, my angel."

When I opened the box, I saw a diamond-studded angel on a silver chain.

"May you always wear it and think of me." Gus came around the table and fastened the necklace.

"Oh, my love. It is too beautiful for words. I will never take it off."

He bent down to me kiss me so gently. It was the perfect ending to a perfect week.

I never took the necklace off, even against the protestations of the doctors and nurses when I had surgery years later.

With Gus receiving the commission for President Garfield's monument, I spent many days at the studio modeling for it. Louis was very involved in the execution, and it was wonderful to be working with him again. The monument was a bust of the president on an upright slab called a stele. In front of it was a statue symbolizing the Republic, for which I posed. I held a shield in front, covering most of my body. Just a little of my left foot appeared from underneath the folds of my gown.

The shield was one way to hide my body, which no longer had its youthful curves. I tried to capture the look of an angel guarding the country's freedoms. Gus encouraged me to think in terms of a strong and wise woman protecting the Republic she believed in.

James Garfield Monument was unveiled in May 1896 in Fairmount Park to a large crowd of thousands. The Stars and Stripes flag was draped over the statue. There were incandescent lamps, electric lights of various colors, and flowerbeds creating a luminous and beautiful reflection of colors. A flotilla of singers, dignitaries, and Japanese lanterns drifted by on the nearby river. The First Regiment and Battery A marched in a procession led by prominent generals.

I wish I could have been there, but I could no longer risk being recognized by Gussie or any of the family. With great enthusiasm, Gus later shared every detail about the event and how receptive the people were to his masterpiece.

For the first few years Louis went to school, it was still hard to be apart from my little boy. But I soon realized he was a quick student who learned his lessons well, even teaching me some simple bits of history and math. Sometimes we would give each other a spelling test. His teacher assured me he was a good student who did not misbehave.

But in other ways, his school years were not always easy for him or me. The distance between Aspet in Cornish and our home in Darien was not enough to quiet any rattling tongues, even after several years. Louis was exposed to unkind prejudice and cruel remarks at school. He had only a couple of friends, but mainly kept to himself.

Louis had questions himself. He knew he was not "like the other kids" in having a traditional family of a mother and father living together in marriage. Our little story of Papa being a traveling salesman did not fool Louis. He overheard and saw things, quickly figuring out the truth.

One day when he was about seven, he and I had a long talk about Papa and me. He listened and asked only one question: "Do you love each other?"

"Of course we do. We love each other very much."

"Then why don't you get married?"

I smiled and ran my hand through his thick hair. "Oh, if only it were that simple. Someday you will understand. But right now, it is important that you know we love you and are always here for you."

Louis was shy and quiet and took the bullying and teasing at school without any fighting. Gus tried to teach him how to box or punch.

"Hold your arms up like this." "Now keep moving your feet." "Keep your eyes on your opponent's eyes." These were the types of instruction Louis heard. However, it was not in my sweet boy's nature to fight. Rather, he was one to retreat into himself.

"What is wrong with that son of yours?" Gus would complain. "He needs to learn to be a man."

I had no answer for such ridiculous words. The only men from whom Louis was to learn about life were his father and Uncle Louis. They were the same kind of gentle souls. I did not know why Gus would try to make Louis a fighter when he himself was not one.

Chapter 20

Paris

1897–1900

For *Sherman Monument*, Gus used three models at various times, including me. Another model was Alice Butler, a lovely young woman who lived in Windsor, Vermont, not far from Cornish. The other was Hettie Anderson, a young black woman who was quite beautiful. Gus used our features to create the look of the angel leading Sherman on to success. This particular aspect of an angel leading the general did not sit well with the Southerners who were still suffering from their defeat and the freedom of the black slaves.

Gus was not as strong and vibrant as usual during this time, yet he worked very hard and long hours on this monument. He worked on it in New York, Paris, and Cornish, always trying to capture the essence of Sherman as a man and a hero.

Gus worked and reworked the angel, known as Victory, many times until he saw the same kind of look and face as was on *Amor Caritas*. I was frequently at the Twenty-Seventh Street studio posing for this angel that symbolically led Sherman. I listened carefully to Gus's descriptions of how he wanted Victory to look. One day I sat quietly, and with my eyes open wide, I focused on an area of the opposite wall. I went into a trance-like state, recalling when a fairy visited me in the Hoboken woods. Using thoughts only, she advised me how to rise above my fears and insecurities. From her I had heard the familiar words: *Follow your heart. Follow it with unconditional love.*

I believe Sherman too had followed his heart by helping bring the country together and helping free the slaves. He and his angel were one and the same with their goals.

Then suddenly the trance was broken as Gus took my hand. He gently murmured, "Davida, that was perfect. Your face reflected exactly what I was trying to achieve."

After fourteen years, *Shaw Memorial* was unveiled on the wet, drizzly day of May 31, 1897. It was considered one of Gus's finest works. He had strived to capture the individuality of each man so that his story appears to be told. The black soldiers' role in the Civil War was not to be underestimated or ignored, and that was why Gus was meticulous in his endeavors. Gus also had reworked the angel several times, which contributed to the long delay of the memorial being completed. He wanted the angel to be just right, conveying the message of her guidance and protection.

Typical of Gus, he did not want to be the center of attention and tried to stay out of sight during the unveiling ceremony. There was a parade that included some of the men of the Fifty-Fourth Massachusetts Volunteer Infantry. After the unveiling, everyone gathered in the Boston Music Hall to hear speeches from various dignitaries, including Booker T. Washington. The memorial was received with great acclaim.

Gus wrote to me of his struggle with depressing thoughts and lack of energy or interest. He wrote, "Will I ever pull out of these melancholies, which I cannot seem to shake off?" He shared how he still had occasional bouts of stomach pain but was not seeking medical advice. "The pain will pass," he wrote.

Worried, I wrote to him that he must see a physician—or do something to address the pain. "If anything, get away for a while and seek out fun and relaxation," I pleaded in my letter.

And so he did. He and Alfred Garnier, a long-time friend from their student days in Paris, traveled to the south of France. Gus was able to visit Aspet, where his father was born and raised, and Salies-du-Salat, where his father spent his first years learning shoemaking. In Aspet, Gus met his cousins and the townspeople who knew his family. And in Salies-du-Salat, he saw the name "Saint-Gaudens" above a door for the first time. He was thrilled and felt a new sense of energy and determination.

The two friends traveled on down to Rome, stopping in Nice, then on to Naples and Florence. The ten-day trip did him well. He returned to Paris with renewed spirits.

I was relieved to receive postcards that showed Gus's humor and enthusiasm for life again. The ones from Aspet were most touching as he wrote about this beautiful and friendly town from which his father came. There was a new sense of pride and optimism appearing in his words.

One of Gus's most prized students was a delightful young lady from Ohio named Annetta Johnson. The aspiring sculptor and artist had studied at the Art Students League under the tutelage of Gus. She later went to Paris to continue her studies with him. In time, she and Louis fell in love.

Gus and I were so happy that his brother had fallen in love with such a very sweet and kind lady. When I saw them together once they came back from Paris, it was obvious how much they loved each other. I saw a contented Louis, who was truly at peace with his life.

They were married in New York City in 1898, but unfortunately I could not attend the wedding. Rather, I took in every word as Gus described the special day to me.

He got tears in his eyes and expressed with deep emotion, "I am so happy for my brother. I wish our father could have lived long enough to see this day."

I took my kerchief and wiped his tears as he went on to say, "I hope someday it will work out for us to be together forever as husband and wife."

The months passed so quickly, it seemed. Before I knew it, it was September and Louis's ninth birthday. Gus was in Aspet most of the time and needed to be there for Homer's birthday. That meant it was just Novy and me together on this special day. I tried to not show my disappointment. I still planned a birthday party for him without his papa. Mother and Ingrid would join us.

Our morning started off with Ingrid and I going up the stairs into Louis's bedroom to sing "Happy Birthday" and bring his cake and requested breakfast. Louis chose exactly what he wanted to eat that whole day, and I made sure to meet his every wish. I made him a raspberry cream cake four layers high—his favorite.

That afternoon, the four of us boarded the train and traveled to the Bronx zoo. It was a lovely experience to see so many animals. Louis said the lions were his favorite because they were the mightiest. Tired and hungry, we arrived home to eat Louis's favorite—Swedish meatballs—followed by some cake and ice cream.

I told him, "Louis, never forget that you are half Swedish—and we Swedes know how to celebrate!"

That night, Louis gave me a big hug and thanked me for such a nice day. I stood back, looked at him, and said, "My goodness. Look how tall you have gotten and how short your pants are." We started to giggle. "We shall go into the city tomorrow to get you some new trousers, Would you like that?"

Louis smiled and said, "Let's buy you a new dress also." His cheeks turned rosy red, and he lowered his eyes while saying, "You are the most beautiful mother in the world, and you deserve a new outfit for the approaching winter."

I reached over and hugged him with all my love pouring out to him.

In late May of 1899, Novy and I traveled to Paris. I did not know how long we would be there, but I looked forward to seeing the city that Gus loved so much.

Initially, I was quite overwhelmed with the language, the size of the city, and the magnificence of all the buildings. There were palaces, large gardens, the Seine winding its way through the city, and the astonishing Eiffel Tower.

Gus had arranged for us to stay at the Hôtel du Louvre for a few days. It was a beautiful and luxurious place centrally located in the heart of Paris. Louis and I easily walked to the Eiffel Tower, the Louvre, and the beautiful Tuileries Gardens.

Later we moved into a small apartment in the Saint-Germain-des-Prés area, which was on the Left Bank of the Seine. We often walked around the Luxembourg Gardens, with its beautiful trees, flowers, and very large fountain. Though Gussie was also staying in Paris with Gus, there was little chance we would ever run into each other. It was convenient for Gus to spend time with us.

Paris was beautiful, with its many gardens, picturesque buildings, and outdoor cafés for all to enjoy the warm weather and sunshine. I marveled at the great works of art at the Louvre and the majesty and beauty of Notre Dame Cathedral. I stood in awe of the Eiffel Tower, seeing its beauty and architectural genius.

Louis learned to speak, understand, and read French quite well, thanks to his father, who enrolled him in a French school, called a lycée. Louis did well in school and made some new friends who did not question his family.

One evening, Gus took Louis and me to the opera house designed by Charles Garnier. At first I thought he might be related to Gus's dear friend Alfred Garnier. Gus clarified for me that the two men were not related, just shared the same last name.

For the event, I bought a beautiful gown of gold brocade and white lace, and I purchased a tuxedo for Novy. The opera house took my breath away with the size and opulence of its gold leaf, crystal chandeliers, mosaic tiles, and sweeping stairways. Every detail—the maroon velvet seats, the brass railings, the flooring designs, and the private boxes—was perfect. There was a long reception room with two large fireplaces at each end, a marble floor, and magnificent chandeliers that opened out to a balcony spanning the front of the building.

Both Louis and I later described it as going into a magical world of grandeur not found anywhere else.

Our time in Paris was wonderful in many ways, but when Louis was in school and Gus was working, I was quite lonely. I had no garden, no family, no woods to walk in, and no friends. I especially missed my mother, from whom I had never been so far apart. I tried to read the menus, listen to the people, and ask questions, yet I found the French language very difficult to learn. Some evenings Louis would try to help me read and speak French, but I more often than not got frustrated.

Louis and I had a quiet Christmas together. I tried to make it a special time together but my heart was heavy and lonely without my family and our Swedish customs.

I expressed these feelings of loneliness to Gus.

"I understand, my dear," he said, taking my hand. "Perhaps when Louis is at school, you would be happier if you went out on excursions. There is so much to do or see in Paris."

I shook my head. I had already seen every palace, museum, garden, and attraction. I did not need to see anymore.

"I miss my mother and my home. I want to go back to Noroton Heights," were my words.

So in January 1900, Louis and I boarded a ship bound for New York City after stopping in London. We were glad to be back home. Louis returned to his old school. After attending school in France, Louis told me school seemed easier here in America.

I was anxious to see Maria after being in Paris for what seemed such a long time. Louis and I went to see her one sunny but cold January day.

Maria still had her wonderful sparkling eyes, but her once-erect body was now stooped over, and she walked with a slow shuffle. She was so thrilled to see Louis. She showered him with hugs and kisses.

"Such a beautiful boy—or I should say handsome?" She went to the cupboard and brought out an oatmeal cookie for him. Louis smiled and said thank you.

Next Maria handed him a gift. "This is something that belonged to my husband. I want you to have it."

Louis opened the box, revealing a beautiful pen set with an

onyx base.

"I know you're young, but one day soon you'll go to college. I hope this pen will help you with your studies."

Louis thanked Maria with sincere exuberance. "I will treasure this forever and always think of you."

I smiled as I looked at Louis. I felt such pride in my son. "I think Louis looks more like my father, who had brown hair the color of a roasted chestnut," I beamed. "And Papa was tall and lean with large muscular hands. Papa was always a happy man with a constant smile on his face." I paused. "Though I do wish Louis would smile more."

Louis lowered his eyes and did not respond. I reached out to give him a hug. I understood how our family circumstances affected Louis's personality. Over the years, I had tried to explain things to him, but at eleven years old, he did not fully comprehend or maybe even accept.

Maria and I visited while Louis played the piano in the parlor. We enjoyed the time for uninterrupted conversation.

"I am worried about you, Maria. You live alone here with no one to watch over you."

"Oh nonsense! I'm fine. I don't need anyone watching over me. My neighbors Frank and Sylvia check on me almost every day, though I tell them not to bother."

"I want you to come live with me," I pleaded. "You can have your own room. I have a big yard. You can plant a garden, if you like. You can go for walks in our neighborhood or do whatever you want."

"Oh, don't be silly, my sweet child. You don't need an old lady taking up room in your life. I have my own garden and lots of friends. And I can't leave this place that has been my home for so many years. Oh my goodness—I can't even count how many!"

She laughed and looked at me with warmth and love.

"You've been like a daughter to me. I've treasured our friendship all these years. Your visits and our talks have kept me young and interested in life. But now I know my time here on earth is nearing an end."

I tried to interrupt her with protests, denying the truth.

"Hush," she said gently, taking my hand in hers. "My child, death is just a new beginning, not an end. I will live on in the hearts of those who knew me here on earth. Just as your papa has lived in you, and you teach Louis about him. And I believe my soul will go on to another place. I'm not sure what or where this place is, but I know it'll be a better place than here. So do not cry for me when I'm gone. It's the circle of life. We receive love, give love, and leave love."

Maria passed away two months later on March 23. Her neighbor Frank found her in the kitchen lying on the floor with her shattered teacup nearby. It was one of the dainty teacups with flowers painted on the sides, from which she and I shared so many afternoon teas together.

Frank kindly gave me the complete tea set. "I know she would like you to have them."

The phrase from the Bible "my cup runneth over" comes to me whenever I see or use the tea set. Maria was now one of my special angels—as she had always been.

Maria had no relatives in the area. Most of them had settled out West and had little or no contact with her. I arranged for her to be buried at Spring Grove Cemetery here in Darien so I could watch over her grave.

After the funeral, Louis and I walked to the woods. I tried to instill in him the magic of the trees. In future days, I would teach him about our guardian angels and the true meaning of love.

Gus's health continued to decline while he was in Paris. The doctors found a tumor in Gus's lower intestine, and they wanted to do surgery immediately. But he refused. He sank into a deep depression, using what little energy he had to work on *Sherman Monument* for the upcoming Exposition Universelle in April 1900. At times when the pain was too great, he stayed in bed or rested on a chaise lounge in the studio, giving instructions as best he could.

I later learned his depression became so profound that he considered suicide. In fact, one night he walked toward the Seine, planning on jumping into the river.

"I looked down at the water and decided to take my fate into my own hands. Then I looked up at the beautiful lights of Paris. I began to feel an abundance of love for this city, its beauty, and my work. I knew I had to keep on living and finish what God put me on the earth to do. So I stepped away from the river's wall and with a new resolve walked back to my studio."

Despite the pain and depression, Gus completed his work on time for the exposition. Four of Gus's pieces were on display: *Sherman Monument, Shaw Memorial, The Puritan,* and *Amor Caritas.* Also on display were fourteen reproductions of his relief portraits.

Gus received Grand Prize for *Amor Caritas* and was named a member of the Société des Beaux-Arts and a member of the Legion of Honor. The French government would buy the piece for the Luxembourg Museum.

Of the many artists there at the exposition, Gus was most honored and touched when he saw France's own Auguste Rodin silently standing in front of *Shaw Memorial* with his hat off, giving respect and homage to this great piece of art.

In July, Gus arrived back in New York—accompanied by a doctor. He had surgery in Boston that month. A second surgery occurred in November, also in Boston. He spent time in Florida for initial recovery, then returned to Cornish in mid-December. There he enjoyed the cold temperatures and played in the snow, tobogganing and sledding.

He telephoned me to tell me he was feeling fine. "As a young lad, I missed out on just playing rather than working. Now I am having such fun acting like a kid again!"

My heart jumped for joy hearing his voice so strong and happy. I could not have asked for a greater Christmas gift.

CHAPTER 21

FAMILY CRISES

1901–02

Gus was not the only person in my life with failing health. I could see Mother aging and slowing down from her once-vibrant gait. I worried when I heard her cough, especially at night. Like Ingrid, Mother often stayed with me to help with Louis, especially when I needed to do some modeling.

One early morning, I awoke to Mother's loud coughing, so I arose to check on her. Dawn was breaking, and I found her in the kitchen.

"Mother, are you okay? You are coughing a lot."

"I am fine," she tried to reassure me.

"No, Mother, you are not fine. You must go see Dr. Logan." I could see red spots on her handkerchief when she wiped her pale lips.

A few days later, we learned that tuberculosis was the cause of Mother's coughing; pale, moist skin; and high temperature. Rest, isolation, and medication were the prescribed treatments, but Dr. Logan cautioned us that the prognosis was not good.

Mother stayed with us awhile. Fortunately, it was springtime. The warm and sunny days were beneficial to her. I often set up a comfortable chair in the backyard, wrapped a blanket over her lap, and placed a pot of tea next to her. I had to instruct Louis to stay away from his mormor, which caused both of them great pain. Eventually we moved Mother back to the boardinghouse with Ingrid.

I spent many hours with Mother, encouraging her to stay strong and do as Dr. Logan instructed.

One evening she took my hand and said, "My dear Albertina, I am not afraid of death. My only fear is leaving you at such a young age and with so much responsibility."

Just as with Maria, I tried to protest, but she shook her head and went on.

"I know you do not want to talk about it, but my death is not far away. I will soon be with my beloved Gustaf, whom I have missed so much."

In May, Gus handed me the deed to our Connecticut home at the corner of Hollow Tree Ridge Road and Middlesex Road.

"I know my health is failing. I am feeling well enough now, however, so I want to take care of business," he stated. He took my hands in his, with tears in his eyes. "I want you to have this deed in case anything ever happens to me."

I hesitated. Even knowing about Gus's cancer, I could not bring myself to face the reality of life without him.

"But nothing will ever happen," I protested.

"You silly thing!" he said. "I love your innocence. But truly, I want you and Novy to be secure if anything should happen."

Then in August, he handed over the deed for yet another piece of property in Noroton Heights. I knew then that he had had a premonition. Because of his love, he was trying to protect Novy and me.

In early November 1902, Mother peacefully passed away in her sleep. She wanted her ashes scattered in the woods of Hoboken.

"They are so similar to the ones in Sweden," she had told me. "I know how much you love them."

It was a simple service with a few people from church, many of whom stayed for food and fellowship afterward.

A few days later, Ingrid, Louis, and I traveled back to Hoboken to scatter Mother's ashes as she instructed. The three of us sat quietly on a log. We let the cold November wind gently blow, we watched the gray clouds sweep by, and we listened to the peaceful sounds of the birds, branches squeaking, and squirrels running about. I was at peace. I knew Papa and Mama were together again.

Then complicated thoughts disturbed my peace. Maria was gone. Mother was gone. Only Ingrid remained, though she too was aging. I was now essentially a woman alone with a child to bring up by myself. I was not married to the man I loved. He could not afford to divorce and marry me, his mistress. It might ruin his career, which was, in truth, his first love. Yes, he loved me unconditionally, but his love of creating great works of art was at his very soul. And he now he was stricken with cancer with two families to support. How could I ever make any demands on him?

My home had enough room, so Ingrid moved in with us. She was lonely with Mother now gone. Her presence helped both Louis and me adjust to our lives without Mother.

Life was just getting back to normal when Gus suddenly came to our house while Louis was at school. He greeted me, "I need to speak with you in private."

Gussie had found out about Louis and me. I am not sure exactly when or how, but it had only been a matter of time.

"I had a most difficult conversation with her," Gus told me.

Rightfully, Gussie had been very angry. She had asked Gus to end his relationship with me. But he could not bring himself to leave Louis and me.

I had mixed emotions flowing through me. My heart was heavy for Gus, who had to go through this most difficult situation with Gussie. I knew he did not want to hurt her, yet his love for me did just that. I also felt deep sympathy for Gussie. Her pain and anger reflected how deeply she loved Gus—something I understood well. I myself loved him unconditionally and had all these years. I had not been an honest woman. Such a triangle of love with great sorrow.

Gus decided he would use more caution when he made trips to New

York City or traveled here to Noroton.

"She is off traveling now. I have written to her, promising I will remain discreet and not cause her any embarrassment."

I sat back and let Gus express emotions ranging from anger to hurt to relief.

"She spoils Homer," he groaned, "and I cannot reason with her. She is away all the time for cures or vacations, often taking Homer with her. I get lonely, depressed, and angry." He stopped suddenly and shook his head. "No, it is not Gussie's fault. I am to blame for falling in love with you."

Typical of Gus, he unexpectedly got up and paced the floor.

"You know, Louis has more manners, is wiser with his money, and knows what he wants to do with his life at his age. Compare him to Homer, who is nine years older but still does not know what career to choose. He has no sense about money. He thinks he can just ask for something and get it." He paused and chuckled. "Well, that is because he usually gets what he wants. I think Gussie indulges him because she knows neither of us are happy in our marriage."

"Come and sit down, my love. You are wearing a hole in the carpet."

I looked at him with kindness and concern in my eyes. He smiled and sat down with his hands clasped in his lap.

"Does Homer also know about us?" I asked.

"Yes—unfortunately or not—he does. I am not quite sure how he found out, whether Gussie told him or whether he found out some other way. He confronted us. Gussie and I both had a long talk with him."

"That must have been very difficult."

Gus shook his head. "Well, it was not as difficult as what happened after I took Homer's medallion down and replaced it with the one of Novy. The truth was out about you and Novy, and Homer and I had had a rather fierce argument."

"Oh, Gus," I exclaimed, putting my hands to my lips. "Are you sure you should have done that? That must have hurt and angered Gussie and Homer even more."

"You are right. It only made things worse between us. But at the same time, Novy is my son too. And there is more," Gus added. "Some friends were over for supper, and they asked about some of my pieces of art on the walls. We were walking around looking at them as I explained each one. Then we came to the medallion of Novy. I hesitated, thinking about what to say. Then Gussie hollered, 'Tell us about this medallion!' It was an embarrassing moment. Everyone could hear the rudeness in her voice. I scowled at her, lifted my head, and simply replied it was of one of my sons. Before more could be said, I invited the men to follow me to the parlor for brandy and cigars. Gussie and the ladies stayed in the dining room drinking coffee and tea."

Gus looked at me with eyes seeking approval for his actions that night. I could only nod my head. I put myself in Gussie's shoes—I understood that she was angry but also embarrassed. Even I thought Gus's behavior had been quite childish and disrespectful. I finally just changed the subject.

After the shock about Gussie and Homer learning the truth, I was grateful that many people still supported me. Gus's assistant, Frances Grimes, was very supportive of my relationship with Gus and protective of our privacy. They understood he was very much in love with me.

Louis and Annetta were also quite supportive and spent several afternoons with me. Louis shared how troubled Gus was.

"Davida, he is hurting so much for you as well as Gussie," he went on. "His love for you is deep and true, yet he has a commitment and a certain kind of love for Gussie that he cannot ignore."

Helen Tutschek, my dear friend of so many years, traveled from New Jersey frequently. With Mother and Maria both gone, I relied on Helen's friendship more.

Sometimes we just sat and let the stillness of the parlor be my comforter. Other times, all I needed was her arms around me as I cried and shared my fears. Her friendship was always there for me.

There were many days I found comfort just sitting outside under the large pine tree in the backyard, where I found solace and support. One day as I was leaning against the pine tree, I went into a dream state. I heard the tree whisper words of comfort and felt its arms wrap around me. Its spirit whispered, "Let go of fears and trust God. Let His angels guide you. Your life is important and precious."

Then I awoke from my dream, which was not a dream at all. It was the way God and I communicated, just as Papa always had done with God.

CHAPTER 22

LIFE AND DEATH

1903

The year began with Gus spending more time in Cornish. I missed him and continued to be concerned about his health. In his letters, he talked about "my energy often failing me now when I need it the most. My appetite is not good, and the food I used to enjoy is no longer appealing. Just as in other times I struggle with melancholy and feelings of emptiness." It broke my heart that I could not be with him all the time. He and I would meet in New York City as often as possible, or sometimes he came to Connecticut. I always missed him and never felt I had enough time with him.

Gus was busy working on *Sherman Monument*. He had set it up outside in a field. He also bought a horse so he could observe its movements: What did its legs look like when trotting or standing quietly? How did its neck muscles look? What was the flow of its mane?

Gus had made several sketches and a bust of Sherman several years ago. Now he concentrated on putting all these factors together to make a statue Sherman would have approved of. He wanted it to show that Sherman was a kind, brilliant, and brave soldier and leader.

On May 30, *Sherman Monument* was unveiled at the Grand Army Plaza at Fifth Avenue and Fifty-Ninth Street in Central Park. Novy and

I attended the ceremony, watching from the crowd.

When the veil was removed, the applause was thunderous. We heard words of praise all around us. For ten years, Gus had put his heart and soul into the statue—and it showed. Gus had brilliantly shown Sherman as the brave and legendary figure of the Civil War. Victory guided him with her forward movements and determined face.

We watched while Gus stood on the platform yet tried to stay out of the limelight from the other dignitaries. Unlike at other unveilings, there were automobiles instead of horses and buggies. There was a parade, including some of Sherman's soldiers, and the mayor and the Secretary of War, Elihu Root, gave speeches.

After everyone left, Novy and I made our way up to the statue and walked around it. Novy looked at the horse closely.

"Mama, the horse looks alive, as if it will suddenly jump off the base and run off with Sherman."

I laughed in agreement with Novy's assessment. I put my arm around my son's shoulders.

"Your papa is a very gifted artist. Everyone wants him to do some work for them. He always has so many projects, from large statues to small medallions. That is why we do not see him very often, but we are very proud of his work."

Not long after that happy news came some difficult and sorrowful times. It appeared that, my dear aunt Ingrid was rapidly declining. I think she missed her husband and sister and was ready to leave this life.

Ingrid was often confused and forgetful, which worried both Louis and me. One time Novy came home from school and smelled gas as soon as he entered our home. Running to the kitchen, he found an empty pot sitting on a burner that had been turned on but not lit. Fortunately, he knew to quickly turn off the gas, open all the windows, and fan the air to disperse the fumes. He found Ingrid sitting on the bed. She surprised him with the question, "Hello, and what might be your name?"

The next day I took Ingrid to see Dr. Logan, who diagnosed her with advanced dementia. For everyone's safety, he recommended we put her in a local home for the aged. I knew he was right, but I agonized over the decision. My dear son, being wise beyond his years, encouraged me to think about Ingrid's safety.

"And what would she say if she could make the decision herself?" he asked.

Two days later, I gave Ingrid a hug, promised to visit her soon, and whispered in her ear, "I love you." Then I tearfully left her at the home for the elderly. Louis and I went to see her twice a week. Each time, we noticed her slowly regressing.

She died three months later in early September —alone with no family by her side.

I felt guilty. But as Louis reassured me, "Mother, she never seemed to know if we were there or not. Besides, she is in a better place now."

Novy was right, of course. But it was hard to come to terms with how she had lived her final years. She had always been one to help and encourage others first, putting her dreams and needs second. She left Sweden so her husband could pursue his dream. Then she suffered through several miscarriages and was never able to have children. She buried her husband at a young age. She gave up the farm she so loved and lived in a city that never truly seemed like home to her. And then she buried her beloved sister a short time later.

She had always said she wanted to be buried next to Nels. The day we buried her was sunny and bright. A gentle warm breeze filled my heart with peace and acceptance. I was pleasantly surprised to see Gus standing by an old oak tree, trying to stay out of sight. I simply nodded as Louis and I walked by.

"I am so glad your papa came here today. Our dear Ingrid truly liked him and often told me how he was always very kind to her."

Three very dear people had passed from this life. They left behind their spirits of love, service, and kindness. But I still felt a large void, especially as I considered Gus's health as well. It made me contemplate many questions about life and death.

Though I grew up in the Lutheran church and followed its teachings, one thought had always haunted me: The church did not teach about the fairies and dwarves that I and many of my people believed in. Were we wrong in our beliefs?

And over the years, I had learned about other religions, and it came to make sense to me that there is more than one life, one death, and one way to what is called heaven. Can it be true that the only ones who go to heaven are those who believe in only Jesus? What about all the good people who live with love and kindness but follow Buddha or some other great teacher?

Gus and I would talk about this very subject often. He had addressed the same questions, especially while working on the Adams memorial.

"I studied Buddhism and Michelangelo's work in the Sistine Chapel, trying to capture the essence of death, hope, grief, and spirituality," he sighed. "I do believe there is far more to life and death than what we mere mortals have any concept of."

I had many thoughts about my own mortality as well. Sometimes I worried I would be punished in hell, as taught by the Lutheran church, for being Gus's mistress. But then I knew that I was not just a mistress—we were two people deeply in love.

One day I went to the nearby woods and quietly sat among the trees. I prayed for Papa and Mama to come and speak to me.

I cried out, "I feel so alone and I am scared. Please help me!"

The trees began to sway, and the leaves fell slowly and gently laid upon the ground around me. I could hear voices behind me, and when I turned, there my parents stood side by side in radiant light.

"You are never alone, Albertina. We are always with you. Do not be afraid because love will see you through. You have work to carry on through your son."

Slowly, their images faded, and all I could see were the trees standing straight and tall.

I whispered, "I must stand straight and tall from now on and walk with only love in my heart."

The New England Society of Philadelphia commissioned Gus to do another statue of Samuel Chapin, the subject of *The Puritan*. This new statue was to be dedicated in City Hall Plaza. Gus made some changes to *The Puritan* and named the newer version *The Pilgrim*. He changed the face slightly and titled the book the Holy Bible. The statue was well received.

Nettie and Louis surprised me with a visit one spring day in May. They brought with them their son, Paul, who was now an active four year old. We sat out in the backyard in the shade of the pine tree. Novy and Paul ran around playing tag. We laughed as Novy let little Paul catch him.

"We wanted to see you and share some exciting news," Nettie said with a sparkle in her eyes. Before I could say a word, she went on, "Gus has sold to us—or actually given us—some land just up from Aspet."

Louis quickly interjected, "It is over four acres of land. Now that Nettie and I are both working at the studio, it is the perfect solution to our housing situation."

I listened as they went on to describe their plans for their new home. I was delighted for them. Yet at the same time, I was a bit jealous. I wished I were the one living at Aspet with Gus, with my dear Nettie and Louis next door.

Hearing Paul's loud giggles as he ran into Nettie's arms brought me out of my reverie.

"I am so happy for you," I said sincerely. "How kind and generous of Gus."

They stayed for lunch, complimenting me on the delicious meal of sausages, boiled potatoes, and fruit. The simple meal was topped off with some tea and chocolate cookies.

CHAPTER 23

GOLD COINS

1904–05

A terrible tragedy occurred at Aspet in October when a fire erupted in the barn, destroying much of Gus's studio, letters, photographs, and casts. The *Seated Lincoln* Gus had all but completed it and now it was in total ruin. But as he later related to me, his greatest loss was a drawing he had made of his mother. Another damaged sculpture that had been in progress was of Charles Parnell, one of Ireland's great leaders. Gus was determined to complete the sculpture in a timely manner and have it recognized as one of his masterpieces. This was in honor of his mother and his own place of birth.

The night of the fire, Gus was attending the theater in New York, and Gussie was at a friend's home for supper. All the servants had left Aspet to enjoy an evening off. Neighbors saw smoke coming from the direction of Aspet and rushed to put out the flames. Gussie arrived as soon as word got to her.

When Gus returned home and saw the devastation, he cried. But by the next day, he was planning and organizing to build a new studio and work on his lost sculptures.

Gussie felt guilty and responsible for what had happened, though everyone tried to reassure her that the fire would have happened whether she had been home or not. Still, she had to get away. She traveled to Saint Louis and New Mexico.

It had been five years since Maria passed away in 1900, but she was never far from my thoughts. One afternoon I was drinking some tea from one of her cups, enjoying the warmth of the fireplace on this cold January day. I was resting my head on the back of the chair, when suddenly I heard Gus's booming voice break into song. I opened my eyes and laughed as I watched him do a little dance while he sang. At last, he tired out and sat down next to me.

"Phew! I am not as young as I used to be. That little dance wore me out," he gasped. After a few moments, he caught his breath and went on to say, "I have some very exciting news to share—I wanted to tell you in person. Is Novy here? I want him to hear the good news too."

I smiled at his childlike exuberance, then explained that Novy was in town inquiring about a job at Fitch's Home for Soldiers. "He wants to earn some money to save for MIT. He will be sixteen this fall. He has become a handsome, responsible, and bright young man."

"Does he not know I will pay for his education?" Gus interrupted. "However, it will be good for him to learn about earning his own money and how to work for other people. I am proud of him."

"If you can stay for a while, you can tell him that yourself. He should be home around five." I saw Gus begin to shake his head, so I pressed on. "I have a lamb stew cooking ever so slowly. I know how much you love it. Surely you can stay for that and a chance to spend time with Novy, whom you have not seen in quite some time."

There was a long silence. I knew Gus was trying to figure out how he might delay his return to Cornish.

"I had promised Louis I would come up to Aspet today so we could work on some of the projects that were destroyed in the fire." He smiled and shook his head. "Well, all that can wait. I *will* stay for that lamb stew and enjoy my time with you and my dear son. And I shall announce my exciting news to you both."

Just then, Novy came in with a bounce to his step and a broad smile. He greeted his papa, then walked over to give me a kiss on the cheek. Standing straight and tall, he looked at both of us.

"I have great news! I was hired to work every day for two hours after school and all day on Saturdays at Fitch's. I will help take care of the soldiers by pushing their wheelchairs or walking next to them in case they need assistance." Novy smiled and said, "I will be trained to do a variety of things. This is work where I can help others."

Gus and I both congratulated him, then Gus went on to discuss with Novy the importance of a good work ethic and the sense about handling one's own finances. I treasured watching and listening to the conversation between a father and his son. It was a rare moment.

Novy did not look like Gus but had his intelligence and drive to do the best he could. I watched my son sweep his hand through his dark hair and nod as his listened to his father. His nose was fuller, but he had Gus's green-gray eyes. He also had a quieter, more stoic personality from his Swedish side. I believe at times he felt intimidated by Gus's boisterous demeanor. I saw this so clearly as I watched Gus do most of the talking while Novy gave his father respectful attention.

"I have some news also," Gus announced. He paused for just a brief moment, then proudly stated, "The Inaugural Committee wants me to design a commemorative coin for President Theodore Roosevelt." Gus looked at each of us smiling. "But I have more to share. Our own president called me and wants to meet with me as soon as possible. He wants me to design two coins for our currency—a ten-dollar and a twenty-dollar gold coin. He also wants me to design a special one-cent coin." He excitedly got up from his seat and stood before us. "Can you imagine that? The president of the United States called me. I could not believe it. I am still a little surprised!"

Immediately I glanced at Novy. I could see in his eyes and his whole body that something had changed in him. I knew what it was. Novy was so proud of his new job, yet his father had to do or achieve something even more important. My son and I had always lived our lives on Gus's schedule, needs, and accomplishments. It was a price I was willing to pay because of my deep love for him. However, it seemed unfair that my son would have to live in the shadow of his very successful father.

I knew I had to find a way to explain this to Gus. The opportunity came when we were lying in bed just holding each other. I very careful with the words I chose and my tone of voice.

At first Gus was quiet. Later on, he nodded, "I understand how selfish and self-centered I was. I am sorry. I will apologize and talk to Novy in the morning."

"I know Novy is proud of you," I insisted. "However, he is at an age and time of his life when he is trying to accept who and what our family is and has been. He has had to lie about his family, and he knows what society calls people like him." I started to cry. "He and I have had many talks, but I do worry how our love has affected him now and for the future."

We fell asleep in each other's arms. Our times of lovemaking had waned, especially after his two surgeries, yet our days together were still sacred to us.

I knew our time was limited, and I believe at some level he did too. He was living the only way he knew how, and that was to spend as much time as he could with both of his families.

His families were growing, actually. In June, Homer married a young lady named Carlota. Wedding preparations had been going on for a year, with Gussie in charge. Gus told me he was happy for Homer and liked Carlota.

"She will be a stabilizing force for my son who needs to bring some structure into his life," he said.

That summer I seldom saw Gus, and when I did, he was quite excited about his plans for the coins commissioned by President Roosevelt. He designed the commemorative coin with an eagle, using the same design as he did for the *Shaw Memorial*. Roosevelt's profile was on the other side. Unfortunately, the coin was never minted under the United States Mint and did not receive the recognition it deserved.

"I have had many discussions with the president about the other coins. We have exchanged ideas and sketches of eagles and figures of Liberty," he conveyed to me when we met briefly at Delmonico's for supper.

I smiled at him. "I am so proud of you, Gus. To have the president of the United States requesting you to do these coins is such an honor." I lifted my glass of wine and toasted him, "Skål."

Gardening became an ever more important part of my daily life. I planted white roses around a birdbath. I had an arbor built with a white bench, and I planted purple wisteria to climb over it. Clipping back plants and pulling weeds were like removing the sad things in my life. New plantings were symbolic of the joys. And watering was a reminder to nurture myself every day. I also still found solace and inspiration as I went to the nearby woods rather frequently.

Once a month, I traveled to Hoboken to visit my family's gravesites, then I would visit Maria's at Spring Grove Cemetery. I often invited Nettie or Helen to go with me. We would make it a special time to remember those who had passed but also to celebrate our friendships.

CHAPTER 24

MORTALITY

1906

In March, Gus had two operations, of which Uncle Louis kept me informed about through letters and visits. "I am worried about him, and I am working as hard as I can helping him with his many projects," he wrote. "You know that he will never stop until he takes his last breath."

I could sense that the strain of worry and work was taking its toll on Louis as well. Nettie's influence and love kept him from drinking to get through these difficult times.

Gus came to New York and stayed at the Player's Club while having x-ray treatments to ease his pain. I was with him as often as possible. He was thin and somewhat gaunt looking, yet his effervescent smile was there.

On one particular visit with Novy and me, Gus said, "I have been remembering the times of my childhood with great joy. I was blessed to have such a kind and loving family." He looked straight into Novy's eyes, saying with a crack in his voice, "I hope someday you will look back at your childhood the same way."

Novy did not say anything. He kept his eyes cast down and slightly nodded.

At home that evening, Novy said, "Mother, you are my family, not Papa. I am sorry if this hurts you, but it is the truth. I deeply care about him, but my memories of my childhood will always be with you, Mormor, Aunt Ingrid, and Maria."

I wiped away some tears and whispered, "I know. I know."

In June, tragedy came into the lives of so many. Harry Thaw, a jealous husband, shot Stanford White to death. Stanford had had an affair with Thaw's wife, Evelyn Nesbit, a few years earlier. Evelyn was a sensation as a model and an actress. She was but sixteen when Stanford was involved with her.

Over the years, Gus's friendship with Stanford had gone through some changes. They were not as close as they had once been. Still, Gus was deeply affected by Stanford's death.

"I do not know if I can ever work with another architect," he said. "He was the finest."

While Gus's health was failing, the energy he put into his work was as passionate as ever. Gus had many ideas for the designs of the two gold coins and a one-cent piece. His passion for this project was unlike any other. I think he knew it would be his last and also one of his most famous accomplishments.

Gus and President Roosevelt had several more discussions and exchanges of ideas. There were many letters and a few meetings between them, each expressing what he thought was important.

For the ten-dollar gold coin, Gus developed over seventy different variations, then narrowed it down to twenty. He asked friends and colleagues which they liked best. Gus used the inspiration of Victory's head, then added an Indian headdress, which President Roosevelt had insisted upon. Gus added forty-six stars milled around the edge to represent the number of states in the Union.

The twenty-dollar gold piece featured Liberty holding a torch in her right hand and an olive branch in her left. She was striding with a display of determination, her left leg forward and her foot resting on a rock. On the reverse side, an eagle was flying from right to left with rays of the sun shining under the wings. There were thirteen stars for the original colonies and *"E Pluribus Unum"* without "In God We Trust"—

which caused an outrage.

The one-cent piece featured a woman's head with an olive wreath in her hair. Thirteen stars appeared above her on one side. On the reverse side was a flying eagle like the one on the 1857 penny.

The one-cent coin was never minted, and it was a challenge to mint the two gold coins with their intricate designs. It took the efforts of many, especially Charles Barber, the mint engraver. The coins would finally be minted the fall of 1907.

Gus would never see them.

By the spring of 1907, my only contact with Gus was through letters he sent with Uncle Louis, our secret messenger. He did not trust the mail system to be discrete with letters addressed to a "Miss Davida Johnson Clark." Nor did he trust a telephone call that might be overheard.

I so enjoyed the cartoons and silly poems he sent with some of his letters. Other letters detailed his despondency, his loneliness for Novy and me, and his sadness at his loss of energy. He wrote that he often sat on the porch at Aspet and gazed out at the Ascutney Mountains. "I look at these mountains, and they remind me of the Pyrenees, where Aspet is. I feel a closeness to my father and my French heritage when I recall my visit to that delightful little town."

Uncle Louis also gave my letters to Gus without Gussie ever knowing. When Louis visited, he would share with me how Gus's body was getting so thin. "I think he is disappearing before my very eyes," he said. "Since early childhood, he has been my protector, helper, and inspiration. What will life be like once he is gone? What will happen to us all?"

I too had been struggling with those questions ever since I heard about Gus's cancer diagnosis. What would happen to us all? I frugally saved any money I had made from working, but there was no doubt that I was dependent on Gus for financial support. At least I would be able to keep the house, thanks to Gus's generosity in signing over that deed and a deed to another property a while back.

"Do you think there is any chance I could see him once more?" I asked Louis. "I do not want to get you into trouble, but I do think it would be good for both Gus and me to have just a little time together."

"I know Gus would love to see you. I am not sure how we can do it, but let me think about it." Louis sat quiet for a long time, trying to develop a plan.

I gave Louis a kiss on the cheek and looked deeply into his eyes. "Louis, I am sorry. I am asking too much of you. I am so grateful for all the things you and Nettie have done for me. If God wants Gus and I to meet one more time, then it will happen."

A month later, I received a telegram from Gus: "Arriving on 1:00 pm train June 10—meet me at the Waldorf." I was elated and grateful to Louis, who had made the arrangements for this to happen.

When I knocked at the door of Gus's hotel room, I took a step back, seeing him for the first time after so many months. His once-full head of hair and beard were now thin, and I could easily feel his ribs when we embraced. His arms did not have any strength, and his hands were not as strong. Once I was inside the hotel room, we embraced again and exchanged kisses.

"Come sit down," he said. He guided me to a settee of green velveteen. "Let me just look at you, my amor caritas. You are just as beautiful as ever." He reached up and wiped my tears with his handkerchief. "Do not cry, my sweet. I am fine now that I am with you."

I took his hands and kissed each finger, then put my head in his hands. We shared tidbits of our daily lives.

"Novy has been accepted at MIT. I am so proud of him." I looked intently at Gus and wanted to share everything I could about our son. "He is a handsome, kind, and intelligent young man, Gus. He sends his love but chose not to come today. He wanted us to have our time alone and uninterrupted."

Gus cleared his throat and groaned, "I wish I had spent more time with both my sons. I do not think I have been a very good father."

I tried to interrupt him, but he kept talking.

"Do you remember the deeds I gave you a few years ago? You own those properties free and clear. You can sell them or rent them out. They are good sources of income for you."

"Oh, Gus, I do not care about any of that. Somehow we will get along fine."

But Gus was intent on talking about things that were obviously preying on his mind. As painful as this discussion was, it needed to happen.

"My dear, once I am gone, there may not be any jobs for you. I want you to be more than secure. You know, the world of sculpture is changing. My style is no longer being taught. Rodin and I have often talked about the new art that is emerging."

He scratched his head, and his eyes began to dart around as if he were trying to remember everything. "Now with that in mind, I have made Gussie promise me that she will leave you a home I bought in Arlington, New Jersey. I told her I bought it for you and Novy. If you want to remain living in Noroton Heights, that is fine. Or you can move to Arlington, if you wish. The house is next door to Helen Tutschek's son, Frank Junior."

Once again, Gus showed his loving and generous side. How could I have been so blessed to have him in my life?

We talked, laughed, and cried until the wee hours of the morning as we reminisced about our times together. We soon fell asleep in each other's arms. But once the sun rose, I quietly slipped out of bed, dressed, and left a note next to his coat:

My beloved,

I am not strong enough to say good-bye in person. I should be—we have had so many good-byes in our almost thirty years together. You are always in my heart, and I will love you forever.

All my love,
Davida

Gus passed away on August 3, 1907, with his physician in attendance. Gussie fainted outside the room, and Homer comforted his mother.

Uncle Louis telephoned me. "I am sorry, Davida, but Gus is gone," he cried. "He died this morning."

He handed the phone to Nettie, who said in a broken voice, "My dear Davida, I am so sorry. All I can say is that he is not suffering anymore."

"I know," I said, "and for that I am most grateful." I could hardly speak, though I had known for some time that this day was not far away. "The last time I saw him, he was so frail and had so little strength."

"He taught me so much about the art of sculpture and took me under his wing," Nettie continued. "And because of him, I met Louis, the love of my life." Then she said a statement I will never forget: "The headlines for today's newspapers should be, 'The greatest American sculptor has left this world, but his spirit will live forever in our hearts and his magnificent works of art.'"

Novy came to my side and held me close as I shook with tears of great loss and emptiness. I do not remember that my son cried for his father.

The next day, August 4, there was a funeral at the Cornish studio.

CHAPTER 25

CHANGED LIVES

1907–08

Uncle Louis and Nettie kept in close contact with me. They shared that Gussie was having a particularly difficult time. She was often found sitting in Gus's bedroom, quietly crying. My heart was sad for her and understood her feelings of loss and melancholy. I wondered if she thought about how Gus's death might be affecting Louis and me, just as I thought about her and Homer.

I spent many hours under the pine tree praying for guidance for both Gussie and me. One day I saw Papa and Mama standing together hand-in-hand surrounded by a beautiful light. Their words of love and comfort were conveyed from their hearts to mine.

"Seek solace by sending love to Gussie through prayer. Keep the memory of Gus alive by sharing stories about him with Novy. Continue to remain in the background so as to not cause any stress to Gussie or Homer. Love yourself as the kind and generous woman you are."

I walked back into our home and heard a gentle knocking at the door. I was pleasantly surprised to see Nettie.

"Oh, such a wonderful sight you are," I said with a smile. "Please come in, and let's share some tea."

"Well, I have some news that I think you will appreciate." Nettie sat down and took an envelope out of her purse. "Gussie gave this to Louis, who asked me to bring this to you."

I nervously opened the envelope, which contained a check for $25,000 and the deed to the home in New Jersey that Gus bought for us. I began to shake and could hardly hold the papers in my hands.

"Oh my goodness."

As Nettie explained, Gussie told Louis she wanted to give this to me for two reasons. One, because Gus had asked her to do it, as he had told me at the hotel. And two, because Louis was Gus's son.

The message I had just received from my parents under the pine tree was beginning to come true. I made a vow then that I would live my life as God, Gus, and my parents would want.

I found Novy sitting in his room reading one of his many school-books. He was home from MIT for the weekend. After some small talk, I showed him the contents of the envelope and the message from Gussie.

"Mrs. Saint-Gaudens is an honorable woman, and I admire her for complying with Papa's wishes. Under the circumstances, not many women would do this." Novy frowned." I know how much he loved you, Mother, but I never really understood how he felt about me."

I shared with him my experience under the pine tree this morning. Louis smiled and nodded. He did not seem to believe in fairies, appari-tions, or even God. It broke my heart because I believe we each need to have a faith in something greater than ourselves.

I asked him how he would feel about moving to Arlington, New Jersey. "This house has so many memories," I told him. "It might be good for both of us to live in a new place. We would be a little closer to MIT."

"Mother, I am in favor of whatever you want to do. I am home only on weekends now. After college, I am not sure where my life will take me then. In fact, there's something I want to talk to you about."

Novy invited me to sit down.

"You have been so preoccupied with your worry about Papa. Well, I have met a young lady, and I think I really like her." Louis had a rather shy smile, and his eyes searched mine for a response.

I let out a little gasp of surprise. "Oh my goodness! I am so happy for you, my son. Tell me all about her."

"She lives in Boston with her family, who came to the United States from Saint John, New Brunswick. One day I met her while standing on the corner waiting for a bus. She has a smile and sparkle in her eyes that attracted me right away." Novy looked at me for acceptance to continue. "She reminds me of you, Mother. You both have a zest for life and are so kind to everyone."

I was choked up listening to my son's words and seeing a change in him I had not seen before.

"So when can I meet her?" I asked. "Perhaps she can come for supper next Sunday. What do you think?"

Alida Provan was just as Novy had described. I felt an immediate connection to her. Despite a serious heart condition from rheumatic heart fever, she was strong in her willpower to not let her health keep her from living a full life. She was short and petite but a dynamo of energy and enthusiasm. She was the perfect balance for Novy, who was quiet, shy, and reserved.

My son was growing up in many ways. One day he surprised me by asking me not to call him Novy anymore.

"It is a child's nickname, and I am now a man. With Papa gone, there is no reason to use that name. Besides, I want to be called Louis because my namesake has been more of a father to me."

I was shocked and hurt at first, but I also knew deep in my heart that he was right.

In 1908, Louis and I moved to 51 Stewart Avenue, Arlington, New Jersey. I needed to start a new life without Gus and keep only the wonderful memories of the home we shared in Connecticut. This new location was closer for Louis to come home on weekends from MIT. Just as Gus had stated, the house was next door to Frank Tutschek Junior, son of my dear friend Helen.

I loved this house with its Victorian-style wraparound front porch, swing, and large windows looking out onto the quiet street. The large white house sat on a slight rise with a large front and back yard. Ivy grew on a trellis along the one side of the porch, protecting it from the western sun.

The days were long and lonely with Louis away so much. Weather permitting, I spent hours in the garden planting, weeding, and planting some more. My garden soon became filled with lilacs, hydrangeas, roses, and a small area for vegetables. I put up an arbor along one side covered with morning glories, which led to a small bench and a fountain. It reminded me of the beautiful garden Gus's friend had in New York City, where Gus and I had our first love tryst.

Though Gus was gone, he was still quite alive in my heart. I wrote down my fondest memories of our days together, hoping someday Louis would read them and come to understand his father more.

I also made time to visit Gus's works. On my trips to Boston to visit Louis and Alida, I visited *Shaw Memorial* and recalled the many stories Gus shared about the different Negroes who had posed for him. In New York, I made my way to *Farragut Monument* and *Sherman* Monument, marveling at their majesty and how Gus made them come alive.

I also went to the Metropolitan Museum of Art and just sat for hours in front of *Amor Caritas*, situated outside with the sun shining on her beautiful golden body. Wonderful memories flowed through me, and I would leave the museum with a smile. My soul was soaring with the knowledge that I had played a small part in the creation of some of these great works.

On March 2, 1908, there was a memorial service for Gus at Mendelssohn Hall in New York City. Novy and I went, staying back in the shadows. It was a beautiful service highlighting all of Gus's achievements and contributions to the world of art.

A month later on April 10, the Metropolitan Museum of Art had a special exhibition of Gus's works. Novy and I were among the five thousand people who attended.

Novy and I stood arm in arm watching the crowds. I felt overwhelming pride as I looked at his most significant works on display. I smiled listening to kind comments while people walked by. I looked up at my son, who stood straight and tall. He did not show any emotion, just looked straight ahead.

CHAPTER 26

LAST FOREST VISIT

1909–10

I awoke one morning with a pain in my abdomen I could not ignore. I tried some different home remedies and teas, but nothing seemed to ease the pain. It became increasingly difficulty to eat all my food.

When the pain had continued for a few weeks. Helen advised me to see a physician. The doctor said I was probably going through menopause and not to worry. He gave me an opioid for the pain, which helped but also caused me to sleep a lot.

Louis was very concerned and insisted I go see a specialist at Massachusetts General Hospital, which he arranged. I was very nervous and scared while the doctor asked many questions and did an x-ray and a physical examination.

"Miss Clark, I think you have a problem with your colon," the doctor announced to Louis and me. "Surgery is necessary to correct the problem."

"No, no," I said, thinking about Gus and his colon surgeries. "I do not want any surgery. It does not help." I turned and pleaded with Louis, "It did not help your dear papa."

"Mother, you cannot continue to live in this kind of pain," Louis replied. "You must give surgery a chance."

Back home, Helen also encouraged me to have the surgery. She volunteered to stay with me for however long it might take to get well.

"And what happened to Gus does not mean the same for you," she said. "Be brave and have the surgery for Louis's sake."

One week later, I was wheeled into an operating room. I was still wearing the angel necklace Gus had given me years earlier. I refused to take it off.

Hours later, the surgeon approached Louis and Alida. "Her abdomen was full of cancer," he said. "I removed what I could, but I am afraid her prognosis is not good."

When I awoke, Louis was sitting on my bed, holding my hand. I smiled upon seeing his face. Sweet Alida came up next to him. Then I saw worry in Louis's eyes.

"Mother, the doctor says you have cancer. He did all he could for you."

I clasped the angel necklace. I silently said a prayer for strength.

Louis dropped his head in my lap and cried.

"Oh, my son. Do not cry for me." I wrapped my arms around him, and we just held each other.

A few days later, I returned home. I insisted that Louis return to MIT and finish his schooling, which he refused to do.

"No, I will stay by your side and take care of you, just as you always cared for me," he said.

The next few months were a living nightmare of pain that no amount of morphine could ease. Helen, Uncle Louis, Nettie, and Alida were by my side, helping and relieving Louis so he could rest.

It was September 15, 1910. I dreamed I was in the forest with Papa at my side. The sun's rays broke through the clouds, the smell of pine was strong, and the gentle breeze was cool and refreshing. Suddenly a doe and her fawn appeared before us.

Papa declared, "Do not worry. We mean you no harm. I am just a simple woodsman taking his daughter to her new home, where we will all live together in peace and harmony."

The doe nodded. With tears in her eyes, she said, "I am also taking my daughter home, to where there are no hunters."

I grabbed Papa's hand and looked up at him, wanting to be assured that everything was okay. Papa smiled and nodded his head to the left. "Look at who is here to see you."

There stood Mother glowing in perfect light, standing next to a pine sapling.

"Albertina, it is time to come with Papa and me to your home, where there is no pain or sadness."

I reached out my hand and took a step toward her. But then I was distracted by a bright, pulsating light. Next to the largest pine tree I had ever seen stood Gus.

"It is time to go home, my amor caritas. My love will be with you always."

Suddenly the forest was filled with all the different fairies, dwarves, elves, and älvas that had helped me during my time on earth. I was comforted and knew no fear.

I was at peace.

EPILOGUE

My great-grandmother Davida Johnson Clark (Albertina Hultgren) passed from the earth on September 15, 1910, at the age of forty-nine years. Her death certificate read: *post operative paralysis of the intestine.*

My grandfather Louis knew her happiest memories were when they lived in Noroton Heights, so he chose the Spring Grove Cemetery. She is buried next to Maria Louise Johnson.

Louis and Alida married August 25, 1911. They moved to Palo Alto, California, where Louis attended Stanford University. Louis sold all his mother's properties, dropped out of college to tend to Alida when she was pregnant with their first child, and bought an orange grove in Corona, California.

Louis and Alida had three sons: Murray Albert, Richard Robert, and Louis John. My father, Murray, legally changed his name to Michael St Germain. He lived to the age of ninety-five. He had two daughters, who are the only biological grandchildren: my sister, Joan Katherine, and myself, Karen Ruth. The second son, Richard, was killed in World War II. He had no children. Louis John was born with juvenile diabetes and chose to have a vasectomy, not wanting to pass that gene on to future generations. He and his wife had two nonbiological children: Valerie Louise and Richard Dana.

The legacy of the love affair between Augustus Saint-Gaudens and Davida Johnson Clark disappeared with their deaths. Louis refused to talk about his parents because it was too painful. It is my hope that their love has come alive again through this book.

As art deco and surrealism replaced the age of Romanticism, recognition for Augustus Saint-Gaudens's artistic works began to fade. Many of his contemporaries died within a few years of his death: Henry James, John La Farge, Henry Adams, Charles McKim, and Richard Watson Gilder. One artist from Saint-Gaudens's era who has remained well known is Auguste Rodin. His sculptures had taken on a style quite remote from the Romanticism style. A few decades after his death, his works received their deserved acclaim, which remains today.

The ten- and twenty-dollar gold coins have perhaps kept my great-grandfather's name known at all. Most numismatics recognize his contribution to the world of coins but are not always aware of his other works of art.

THE ETHEREAL WOMAN

Her hands have long fingers
Gracefully touching others with love
She expresses many emotions
As she delicately moves them

Her eyes are like the ocean
Blue-gray with glints of sparkle
Sometimes dark with anger or fear
Or radiant with loving thoughts

Her mouth can be soft
With smiles and kisses
Or tight with loneliness and dread
Yet with laughter it soothes the soul

Her body is lithe and tall
Presenting different postures
While standing long or sitting
Without movement or pause

She is the ethereal woman
Who represents Perfection,
Beauty, and the Mystery
Of womanhood's Spirit

AUTHOR'S REFLECTIONS

I recently traveled to France to see works and places from my great-grandfather's life. In Paris, I went to see *Amor Caritas* at the Musée d'Orsay. Unfortunately, it had been placed in temporary storage to make room for a special exhibition of Rodin's works.

I walked through the Luxembourg Gardens, where my great-grandfather spent many hours. I stood outside the apartment and studio he rented at 3 Rue Herschel.

I stood in front of the Eiffel Tower and marveled that Gus was there when it first opened at the World's Fair in 1889.

Our tour bus drove by the École des Beaux-Arts, but unfortunately time prohibited us from going in.

I visited the beautiful Palais Garnier opera house, which took my breath away with its magnificence. At one point, I stood in the hallway and tried to imagine my grandparents there dressed in all their finery. At that moment, I wished I could have entered a time machine and been there with them.

I went to Aspet in the foothills of the Pyrennes to see where it all began for the Saint-Gaudens family. I saw the house Bernard was born in and was able to walk through it, thanks to a very distant cousin, who still owns it. I met with the mayor of Aspet and several people of the Association les amis d'Augustus Saint-Gaudens, who were as honored to meet me as I was to meet them. My very distant cousin, Francoise Sarradet gave me a tour of the home our two great-grandfathers lived. I shared with them the little I knew about my great-grandparents and my grandfather. You can learn more about our visit at www.augustussaint-gaudens-france-amerique.org.

The beautiful village of Aspet is picturesque, filled with narrow streets, shops, and houses. But I was surprised to learn how few residents of Aspet knew of Augustus Saint-Gaudens and that his start came from his father, Bernard.

I have also seen many of my great-grandfather's works here in the United States. Many years ago, I visited *Adams Memorial* at the Rock Creek Church Yard and Cemetery. It is a very spiritual and moving statue. I spent quite a long time sitting on the bench, just gazing at this haunting figure. I shed tears of sadness for Mrs. Adams, who took her own life; tears for the beautiful work of art done by my great-grandfather; and tears for the message of love I interpreted.

In 1985, my father, sister, and I were invited to attend the Metropolitan Museum of Art's special exhibition and celebration of Augustus Saint-Gaudens's works. It was a very moving and exciting trip to see so many of his works at one time. Dad met with the exposition organizer, Kathryn Greenthal, who interviewed him.

Then in 1987, we visited Gus's Aspet estate, which is now the Saint-Gaudens National Historic Site, in Cornish, New Hampshire. There we met with John Dryfhout, the curator. We left with some questions answered and issues clarified. Mr. Dryfhout was very interested in the little information my father could provide.

During that same trip, we visited *Shaw Memorial* in the Boston Common. All of us stood in awe in front of this large bronze relief. I remember looking very closely at the soldiers' faces, almost anticipating one of them would blink, talk, or glance my way. They appeared so alive.

Another very memorable event occurred when I visited *Standing Lincoln* in Chicago in 1998. A father was there with his ten- or eleven-year-old son. The boy was climbing all over the statue, which disturbed me. My husband asked the father to not let his son climb, explaining that I was the sculptor's great-granddaughter. He just laughed us off. We decided to not pursue further. We waited until they left, then we took in the incredible detail and how alive Lincoln looked.

In 2004, *Hiawatha* was on exhibit at the Minneapolis Institute of Art. I proudly shared that event with two of my grandchildren. Until seeing it, I had not realized how truly large it was, standing tall at seven feet. The pure-white marble was dazzling.

My most prized possession is the bronze medallion *Novy.* I am so grateful that my father entrusted it to me. Every time I look at it, I feel a deep mixture of emotions: sadness, pride, and love. I feel sadness that Gus and Davida's love story could not be bound in legal marriage and sadness that my grandfather suffered all his life being a bastard child. I also feel pride for Gus's artistic talent and for Davida's resolve to raise my grandfather to be such a fine and kind man. And the most powerful emotion I feel is love for Augustus and Davida, my great-grandparents, who taught me what unconditional love is.

Notable Works by Augustus Saint-Gaudens

Hiawatha
Farragut Monument
Shaw Memorial
Sherman Monument
Standing Lincoln
Amor Caritas
Adams Memorial
Novy

PHOTOS

$20.00 gold piece.
In circulation in 1907.

Amor Caritas statue purchased by
the French Government. Now in
D'Orsay Museum, Paris.

Albertina Hultgren aka Davida Johnson
Clark Model and mistress of Augustus
Saint-Gaudens

179

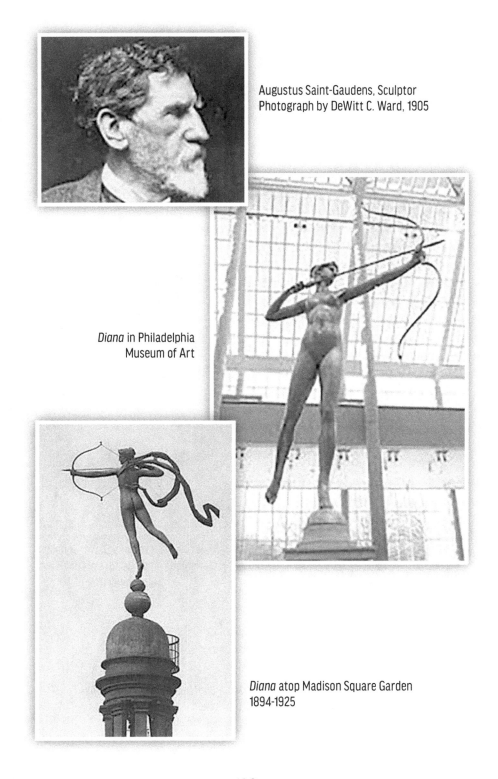

Augustus Saint-Gaudens, Sculptor
Photograph by DeWitt C. Ward, 1905

Diana in Philadelphia
Museum of Art

Diana atop Madison Square Garden
1894-1925

Novy medallion (1892)

Shaw Memorial (1897)
in Boston Common..

Sherman Monument at
entrance to Central Park,
New York City (1903)

Chapter Notes

Chapter 1: New Adventure

Very little is known about Albertina's life in Sweden. There is no clear evidence where in Sweden she was born. When and how Albertina came to America is also unknown. Nor do we know anything about her parents.

There is no indisputable evidence about Albertina's birth name either. It is believed that her last name was either Hultgren or Hallgren. Researcher Monica Eklund Abelsted assisted me in this matter. In a Feb. 11, 2015, e-mail, she stated:

> *I have tried to find Albertina born 1869 in all church books. I also have searched in the emigrant register to find out who took the little girl to USA. Somebody must have brought her, but who did?*

> *But I have succeeded to find the inscription in the church-books of your grand father's grand mother Ludvika Laura Albertina born November 23, 1854 to unknown parents. But it says that the mother was 22 years old.*

> *I found her together with Wilhelm August Hallgren and his wife Sofia Albertina Edelsten, which was 22 years when Ludviga Alma Albertina was born. They call her there foster-daughter and*

her name is often changed in the church-books. Enclose a lot of print screens I have made. Sofia Albertina Edelsten died April 19, 1866, only 33 years old. Wilhelm August Hallgren married then to Sofia Hedvig Theresia Andersson, and they got 3 daughters and one son. Wilhelm August Hallgren died November 12, 1874.

I sent the information above to Dr. Henry Duffy for his opinion and information. He was unable to confirm or deny its accuracy and relationship to Albertina. In an e-mail dated June 18, 2015, he wrote:

The genealogical information you send is fascinating. It may well be related. With Swedish heritage myself, I know it is often difficult to separate names, as the spelling was often variable, and sometimes many people in a village were related, all with different spellings. Of course if you go back far enough you get to the time when there were no last names.

With no clear evidence about Albertina's origins, I used the opportunity to create my own details about the place of her birth, her parents, and how she came to the United States.

Chapter 2: New Land

No one has been able to find evidence about where or when Albertina entered America and with whom she traveled. I chose New York because it was the most common place for European immigrants to enter. Thanks to historical information on the Internet I learned about Castle Garden.

There is no evidence that Albertina believed in the mythological creatures and beings from Swedish folklore. This part of her character was simply inspired by the way I see her. I researched information about gnomes, älvas, and other mythological creatures on the Internet.

The characters Nels and Ingrid Petersson are fictitious. There is no evidence as to where and with whom Albertina lived upon arriving in America.

The Whispering Pines Inn in Hoboken is fictitious.

Chapter 3: Hoboken

Again, there is no information that Albertina lived in Hoboken at any time. This is purely a fictional part of her life.

There is a Maria Louise Johnson buried next to Albertina, but there is no evidence if they were related or knew each other. Struck by the connection of the Johnson name, I created a fictional version of Maria.

My father, Murray Albert Clark, often said he thought Albertina's mother was the cook for Mr. and Mrs. Saint-Gaudens; however, there is no proof.

Chapter 4: Christmas Meeting

I obtained information about Swedish traditions for Christmas and the Festival of Saint Lucia from the Internet. The tradition of the magic walnuts was something my grandfather Louis Paul Clark did for us grandchildren every Christmas. Inside the walnut was a five-dollar bill. I do not know where this tradition came from.

There is no record of any middle name for Albertina.

It is not known how Albertina met Augustus Saint-Gaudens. This meeting is from my imagination. It is well documented, however, that the Saint-Gaudens lived at 22 Washington Place in 1881.

Chapter 5: The Studio

There is no documentation of such a meeting with Gus and Albertina on the road to the inn. Nor is there any evidence that Albertina and her mother went to Sherwood Studios.

Chapter 6: New Career

It is written in several resources that Augusta Saint-Gaudens did have a hearing problem, which caused her to sound harsh.

Louis Saint-Gaudens was an artist and sculptor in his own right. He worked on several pieces independently and with his brother Augustus.

Chapter 7: The Model

Gus did have a studio in the Sherwood Studio Building in 1881.

Several sources refer to Albertina as the model for the Vanderbilt mantelpiece.

Gus did have several affairs throughout his life. Gussie knew about some of them. I included this scene of her meeting with Albertina, though I have not read of their meeting in such a manner.

The friend's home and garden is fictitious.

Chapter 8: The Mistress

There is evidence that Albertina had an apartment at 143 West Forty-Fifth Street.

Frank and Helen Tutscheck were Albertina's friends. Exactly when and how they met is conjecture on my part.

When Gus and Albertina's love affair began is unknown. This scene and place is fictitious.

Chapter 9: New Beginnings

It is well documented that Gus loved opera and classical music. I have in my possession the pearl-handled opera glasses that belonged to Albertina. I only assume Gus gave the glasses to her.

Stanford White and Gus did travel to New Mexico together. There is documentation of their meeting Stanford's brother and visiting the

Harvey House restaurants.

It is well known that Louis did have drinking problems and depression. Gus too struggled with melancholia. However, the meeting with Albertina as described is fictitious.

Chapter 10: New Identity

When, why, and how Albertina changed her name is unknown. I have searched for a name change certificate to no avail. There is question whether she was first just Davida Clark and added Johnson at a later time.

Many resources document that Gus had a beautiful tenor voice and that everyone knew he was happiest when humming or singing.

Chapter 11: Challenges

Delmonico's was and continues to be a popular restaurant in New York City. The scene of Davida and Helen going there for a birthday celebration is purely fictitious.

Gus loved his mother very much and was quite saddened by her premature and unexpected death. How his parents met is well documented.

There is no evidence that Davida ever went to Chicago with or without Gus. I do have a ring that belonged to Davida. How she got it is unknown.

Chapter 12: Lincoln, Shaw, Adams

Resources do document that Gus and Gussie often lived apart.

There was a Young's Hotel in Boston at that time; however, I do not know whether Davida ever stayed there or went to Boston at any time.

Several sources write about Gus's interest in Buddhism and Mormonism as ways to explore spirituality and also to find options out of his marriage.

There are several references that Gus's affair with Davida was a lasting love. It continued for over twenty years. He did explore ways that he might divorce Gussie and marry Davida without hurting Gussie or his career.

Chapter 13: Following the Heart

It is well documented that Gus suffered from stomach pain, indigestion, and melancholia.

It is not known whether Davida ever had to pose in the nude. Because the *Diana* statue is of a nude woman, I created this scenario.

Chapter 14: Diana

My thanks to Monica Eklund Abelstad for translating the Swedish phrase.

Chapter 15: God-Like Sculptor

Amor Caritas is now at the Musée d'Orsay in Paris.

Whether Gus called Davida his *"amor caritas"* is unknown. However, the sculpture is one of his most well-known pieces, and it is well documented that Davida was the only model for it. I can hear him calling her "amor caritas" as an endearing and affectionate name.

Chapter 16: New Birth

It is documented that Gus made a short and unexpected trip to Paris, telling no one except Paul Bion. Because of the timing, many assume he took the trip in order to make decisions about Davida's pregnancy.

The circumstances of my grandfather's birth are not clear, though it is known he was born in New York City. There are no hospital records that I am aware of.

How my grandfather's name was chosen is my conjecture, though Louis is of course Gus's brother and Paul was their father's middle name.

Chapter 17: Novy

Davida was the model for the head of *Diana*, and Julia "Dudie" Baird was the model for the body.

The original *Diana* erected in 1891 was removed from Madison Square Garden in the fall of 1892. The Columbian Exposition Committee bought it and placed it atop the Agricultural Building at the fairgrounds in Chicago. It remained there until February 1894. A fire broke out and destroyed all but the upper portion of *Diana*. In 1909, that portion was displayed at the Art Institute of Chicago. The second *Diana* was installed atop Madison Square Garden in 1894. It remained there until 1925, when Madison Square Garden was torn down. It is now at the Philadelphia Museum of Art.

I have a photograph of Davida's home in Noroton Heights.

My grandfather was given the nickname, or pet name, of Novy. Exactly how that name came to be is still a mystery.

I have a photograph of my grandfather as a young boy sitting on a rocking horse at the house believed to be in Noroton Heights. I created my own story as to how he got this toy.

The *Novy* medallion is in my family.

Chapter 18: Families

Gus did play the flute, and it is now in my sister's family.

Chapter 19: The Bastard

Whether Davida or anyone in her family were great cooks is unknown. It is a creation from my imagination.

I have no evidence that Davida and Gus ever took a trip to Washington, DC, together.

I am sure that my grandfather struggled with not having a traditional family. The Victorian era was very proud and strict, with no regard or compassion for illegitimate, or bastard, children. Even as an adult, my grandfather had no friends or visitors outside the family. He was warm and friendly, yet my grandfather was always afraid someone would find out about his heritage and being a bastard child.

Chapter 20: Paris

Sources disagree on the model for Victory, the angel in *Sherman Monument*. Hettie Anderson, Alice Butler, and Davida are all mentioned.

Annetta Johnson was Gus's student. Louis and Annetta were married in 1898 and had one child, Paul. Louis and Annetta were very close to Davida and my grandfather right up to their deaths. Annetta visited my family in California in the early 1940s. She made a cameo of my sister. She told me I was too young to pose at the time but that she would come back in a year or two to make one of me. Unfortunately, she died before she could return.

Davida and my grandfather did travel to Paris in 1899, but exactly when and how long they were there is not known. My dad talked about his father going to school in Paris and speaking French quite fluently. According to some resources, Davida did not like Paris and was homesick.

The pen set was a treasured possession for my grandfather. On the day he died, it was sitting on his desk at his home in California. I do not know how he came to have it.

Chapter 21: Family Crises

There is documentation of two deeds given to Davida in May and August 1902.

There is no clear evidence as to when Gussie found out about the affair with Davida.

According to one source, the story of Gus showing friends his pieces of art and the *Novy* medallion is true.

Chapter 22: Life and Death

Gus and Gussie did in fact sell almost four acres of land near Aspet to Louis for one dollar.

Chapter 23: Gold Coins

The fire at Cornish and resulting losses are reported in several sources.

There is no information to support the idea that Novy ever worked for the Fitch Home.

My grandfather was an avid gardener, and I believe he would have developed his love and skills for gardening from his mother.

Chapter 24: Mortality

There is no evidence that Gus and Davida met for one last time in 1907 at the Waldorf. I would like to think that they had such a last time together, so I included this passage.

Chapter 25: Changed Lives

The experience sitting under the pine tree is completely from my imagination. I believe my great-grandmother would have prayed for Gussie, tried to keep the memory of Gus alive for her son, and would have continued to live her life with love and kindness. In a May 12, 1965, letter Charles Tutschek, Helen's grandson, stated that Davida "was always so pleasant and full of life."

Chapter 26: Final Forest Visit

According to a letter I received from Dr. Duffy, "Augusta gave Louis $25,000 at his father's death. . . . She reportedly said: 'Because it is his son' referring to Augustus."

Growing up, I heard that my grandfather met my grandmother Alida Provan while in Boston.

The circumstances of Davida's failing health are not clearly known. My grandmother told me how Davida had been in horrible pain and that nothing seemed to relieve it. The word *cancer* was always used.

It is documented that Helen Tutsheck cared for Davida throughout the illness.

Selected Bibliography

Dryfought, John H. *The Work of Augustus Saint-Gaudens.* University Press of New England. 1982. Print.

Duffy, Henry J. and Dryfhout, John H. *Augustus Saint-Gaudens: American Sculptor of the Gilded Age.* Trust for Museum Exhibitions, in cooperation with the Saint-Gaudens National Historic site. 2003. Print.

Gibson, Michael. "Homage to an American Sculptor." *New York Times.* February 20, 1999. Web.

Greenthal, Kathryn. *Augustus Saint-Gaudens: Master Sculptor.* The Metropolitan Museum of Art. 1985. Print.

Hureaux, Alain Daguerre. *Augustus Saint-Gaudens 1848–1907: A Master of American Sculpture.* Somogy Editions D'Art. 1999. Print.

McCullough, David. *The Greater Journey: Americans in Paris.* Simon & Schuster. 2011. Print.

Tharp, Louise Hall. *Saint-Gaudens and the Gilded Era.* Little, Brown and Company. 1969. Print.

Tolles, Thayer. *Augustus Saint-Gaudens in The Metropolitan Museum of Art.* The Metropolitan Museum of Art. 2009. Print.

Wilkinson, Burke. *Uncommon Clay: The Life and Works of Augustus Saint Gaudens.* Harcourt Brace Jovanovich Publishers. 1985. Print.

ABOUT THE AUTHOR

Karen Ingalls is an accomplished and award-winning author. Her first book, *Outshine: An Ovarian Cancer Memoir*, won two awards in the category of women's health.

Her first novel, *Novy's Son: The Selfish Genius*, is about men who seek love and acceptance from their fathers. Unfortunately, they do not always do it using the healthiest of behaviors. This novel is biographical fiction about her father, Murray A. Clark (aka Michael St Germain).

Ms. Ingalls writes a weekly blog at www.outshineovariancancer. blogspot.com, where the subject matter is health and wellness, relationships, and spirituality. Her second blog, www.karensbooks.blogspot. com, is for authors and avid readers. She also has two websites: www. outshineovariancancer.com and www.kareningallsbooks.com.

Ms. Ingalls has several published articles with *Oncology Times, Hormones Matter, Coping with Cancer, PearlPoint,* and *Nursing Forum.* She has written guests posts for a variety of blog sites. She has also been interviewed by *Healthy Living, Rave Reviews Book Club, RNFM Radio,* and *WIMO Radio.*

Ms. Ingalls is a retired registered nurse with a master's degree in human development. She lectures about health and wellness and ovarian cancer.

Links

www.outshineovariancancer.com

www.kareningallsbooks.com

www.kareningalls.blogspot.com

www.outshineovariancancer.blogspot.com

www.twitter.com/KarenIngalls1

www.pinterest.com/kcingalls

www.facebook.com/karen.ingalls.5

www.linkedin.com/pub/karen-ingalls/37/509/ba8

www.goodreads.com/kareningalls

www.amazon.com/Outshine-An-Ovarian-Cancer-Memoir

www.amazon.com/Novy's-Son-The-Selfish-Genius

www.amazon.com/Davida-Model-Mistress

www.plus.google.com

CPSIA information can be obtained
at www.ICGtesting.com
Printed in the USA
LVHW110739260621
691225LV00003B/398